# PECULIAR FIRE

## 10 YEARS OF GUNPOWDER PRESS

All poems are reproduced with the gracious permissions of the individual poets, who maintain copyright for their work. Thank you to the publishers and journals who have allowed previously-published poems to be reprinted here.

Published by Gunpowder Press
Edited by David Starkey and Chryss Yost
PO Box 60035
Santa Barbara, CA 93160-0035

ISBN-13: 978-1-957062-22-8

Library of Congress Control Number: 2025904159

www.gunpowderpress.com

Gunpowder Press is part of Gunpowder Poetry, a 501(c)(3) nonprofit literary organization. The Barry Spacks Poetry Prize is supported in part by the Santa Barbara Poetry Fund under the auspices of the Santa Barbara Foundation.

# PECULIAR FIRE

## 10 YEARS OF GUNPOWDER PRESS

EDITED BY

## DAVID STARKEY & CHRYSS YOST

GUNPOWDER PRESS • SANTA BARBARA
2025

# CONTENTS

# On Creating a New Home for Poetry

by David Starkey, Founding Publisher and Editor

The Gunpowder Press origin story begins on a note of tragedy. A fellow graduate student, David Case—compassionate and yet wickedly funny—came to my rescue when I was lost in the wilds of critical theory at UCLA in the mid-eighties. We were roommates for a time, and though he eventually left Los Angeles for Florida, our friendship thrived right up to the time he died of a heart attack in Gainesville on February 3, 2011, at the age of 49.

David named me as his literary executor, and he left behind a rather jumbled assortment of poetry that eventually became *The Tarnation of Faust*. However, once the collection seemed ready for publication, I could not find a publisher. Repeatedly I was told that no matter how good the poems were, a book by an unknown poet could never find an audience if the poet were no longer alive to promote the book.

Meanwhile, my good friend Chryss Yost, an incredibly talented poet, was still looking for a publisher for her first collection, *Mouth & Fruit*. The stars seemed to align and my long-held desire to become a poetry publisher seemed on the verge of becoming reality.

There was only one problem: I didn't know the first thing about publishing books of poetry.

Fortunately, Chryss's myriad skillsets included the ability to transform a manuscript into a book. She graciously agreed to put her gifts to work for the new press, creating volumes of poetry that benefited from an elegant design vision, one we have retained from our first two books to our most recent.

Of course we needed a name for our new venture. Having just returned from a three month sojourn in Italy, I suggested Dopodomani

Press. But Chryss was never the sort of person to wait until "the day after tomorrow," and she proposed, instead, that we honor our city's namesake, Santa Barbara, the patron saint of, among other things, gunpowder. That settled it: Gunpowder Press we became.

David's and Chryss's books were published in March 2014. Barry Spacks, our friend and mentor, and the first official Poet Laureate of Santa Barbara, had passed in January, and we worked with his wife Kimberley Snow to publish a posthumous new and selected volume of his work, *Shaping Water*, in 2015. We had also known and admired the work of Jim Peterson for decades and were happy to publish his powerful *Original Face* in 2015.

While our initial expenses were bankrolled by royalties from a creative writing textbook I had written, we soon realized we needed more income to keep our nascent press afloat. It felt only natural that we honor the legacy of Barry Spacks with a prize in his name. In our call for manuscripts, we asked only for the "intelligent and accessible" poetry we associated with Barry's work, and we were inundated with wonderful manuscripts, confirming what we already suspected: America is brimming with talented poets.

Our first Spacks Prize winner in 2015 was Catherine Abbey Hodges for her book *Instead of Sadness*. We so admired her work that we've subsequently published two more of her collections: *Raft of Days* in 2017 and *Empty Me Full* in 2024. Catherine's first book was followed by a string of inventive, deeply felt and wildly varied collections: Kurt Olsson's *Burning Down Disneyland* in 2016, Aaron Baker's *Posthumous Noon* in 2017, Michelle Bonczek Evory's *The Ghosts of Lost Animals* in 2018, Glenn Freeman's *Drinking with O'Hara* in 2019, Meghan Dunn's *Curriculum* in 2020, Todd Copeland's *Like All Light* in 2021, Catherine Esposito Prescott's *Accidental Garden* in 2022, and Kellam Ayres' *In the Cathedral of My Undoing* in 2023.

We have been extraordinarily lucky in the insight and good taste of our Spacks Prize judges. Indeed, selections from their work would make a superb anthology of its own: it would include poems by Dan Gerber, Thomas Lux, Jane Hirshfield, Lee Herrick, Stephen Dunn, Jessica Jacobs, Lynne Thompson, Danusha Laméris, and Gary Soto. We also owe a special thanks to our friend Laure-Anne Bosselaar for her unfaltering support of the press and for putting us in touch with so many of our wonderful judges.

Gunpowder Press has always privileged our passion for poetry over commercial considerations, and whenever we felt could break even during the course of a year, we sought opportunities to bring the work of other poets we admired to the reading public. Thus, Nan Cohen's *Unfinished City*, which was a finalist for the 2016 Spacks Prize, became, in 2017, the first entry in what we came to call our Dryden-Vreeland series, open to all K-12 educators and staff, and inspired by two of our favorite and most influential teachers: Michael Dryden in my hometown of Sacramento and Susan Vreeland in Chryss's hometown of San Diego. Christopher Blackman's *Three-Day Weekend*, published in 2024, is the second book in the series.

Peg Quinn had been a finalist in our 2019 contest and was again in 2020, and we published her book *Mother Lode* as an editor's choice that year. Susan Kelly-Dewitt had been a finalist for the Spacks Prize three times: in 2015, 2019 and 2021. Her *Gatherer's Alphabet* became the first book in our California Poets Series, which now includes *Our Music*, the final book by the great Sacramento poet Dennis Schmitz; *Speech Crush*, the penultimate book of poems published by Sandra McPherson in her lifetime; Gary Soto's Covid opus *Downtime*; and *In Praise of Late Wonder: New and Selected Poems* by California's current Poet Laureate, Lee Herrick.

Like Susan, SM Stubbs made our top cut on three occasions—in 2022, 2023 and 2024. After three straight years of loving Scott's work, we knew we wanted to publish *Learning to Drown*.

In 2024, we became a 501(c)(3) nonprofit, and Chryss and I also decided that after a decade of reading tens of thousands of pages of poetry in the process of selecting our contest finalists, that we would, in the future, serve as the final judges ourselves. We couldn't be happier with our initial choices, our first co-winners of the Spacks Prize: Keith Ekiss and Holly Karapetkova. That same year, we began another contest honoring a departed friend and mentor. The John Ridland Poetry Prize is open to poets over 55, and our first winner was Joshua McKinney for his stunning collection *Sad Animal*. Our ten-year anniversary also inspired our decision to bring out a second book by

David Case, *Before Traveling to Alabama.*

Although Gunpowder Press is operated in California by two California natives, we are pleased to have published full-length collections by poets from across the country. Yes, fourteen of our books are by Golden State bards, but we have also published volumes by poets from Florida, Illinois, Iowa, Massachusetts, Maryland, Michigan, Texas and Vermont, as well as two books by New York poets and two by those living in Virginia.

Over the course of our eleven years, we have also been pleased to publish a number of theme-based anthologies featuring work by Central Coast poets, and our Alta California chapbook series, edited by Emma Trelles, has brought the work of Latinx poets, in bilingual editions, to an eager readership. How lucky we have been to publish the poetry of Crystal AC Salas, Nicholas Reiner, Florencia Milito, Gabriel Ibarra, Fred Arroyo, Amelia Rodriguez, and Michelle Moncayo.

If we were to include even a single poem by each of the poets we have published, our anthology would be far too long for our limited means. Therefore, we have decided to focus on work by our poets with full-length single-author collections. We've allotted four pages of poetry for each poet, and while that's a paltry representation of their work, we hope it will compel readers to seek out not only their Gunpowder books, but the full range of their poetic output. As Gunpowder Poetry enters its second decade as an independent literary publisher, our new 501(c)(3) status opens the doors for grants and support from private foundations and donors. We will continue to be a small, independent, hands-on press, but with opportunities to grow and bring more poets to their readers. The books we've published so far are our guideposts.

Keeping a small press alive takes a lot of effort, and Gunpowder Press would never have made it this far without the genius and indefatigability of Chryss Yost, who continues to make each book exceptional, a work of art of that will make both the press and the poet extraordinarily proud.

The spirit of our other founding author also finds itself in our books' pages. The anthology's title comes from the title poem of *The Tarnation of Faust*, in which David Case revisits Charles Gounod's opera *Faust*, with a nod to Hector Berlioz's *The Damnation of Faust.*

Appropriately for a talented classical pianist, David provides a rather detailed description of the music in the opera, yet his title also slyly alludes to a phrase from his Southern upbringing: "What in tarnation is going on?" There's a lot going on in the poem, but ultimately its subject turns out to be Faust's own words, "his peculiar fire and brimstone," and "peculiar fire" seems to us an especially apt description of the magic and mystery of the language of the twenty-five poets in this anthology.

If David were alive to see the enterprise he helped inspire, we believe he would be proud.

DAVID ALLEN CASE

**David Allen Case** was born in Birmingham, Alabama, on July 15, 1961. He earned a Bachelor's degree from the University of Alabama and a Ph.D. in English from UCLA. From the mid-80's through 2011, he taught at several institutions of higher learning, including UCLA, Los Angeles City College, Pasadena City College, Glendale Community College, and Santa Fe College in Gainesville, Florida. He died unexpectedly at age 49 in Gainesville. Case's first book, *The Tarnation of Faust*, was published posthumously by Gunpowder Press in 2014. The publication of *Before Traveling to Alabama* further highlights Case's remarkable talent and marks the tenth anniversary of the Press, which, but for his poetry, would not exist.

# From the Center of the Universe

South Lake Avenue in Pasadena
on Friday in the evening fog
is the epicenter, Cal Tech's seismographs
waiting to etch the magnitude
of some convulsion. Some say the world
will end in smog. I hold with those
who favor flood, like Byron finishing
*Childe Harold*, mourning Shelley
lost in the surf off Malibu, for now
my hands are shaking
and my mind reverts to former centers
of the universe, like Athens, Georgia,
or Lansing, Michigan, one day when
the sun stood overparked, as at Jericho.

Here, neither Bible nor *Das Kapital*
can harm me, though who knows what
the Eminem spewing through the windows
of this red TransAm portends.
In the listening booths of Tower,
I evaporate in songs without words,
the muted turbulence of jets, freeways,
and helicopters humming in my bones.

## As the World Turns

Someone is playing (and maybe overpedaling)
"The Poet Speaks," the very last
Of Schumann's *Scenes from Childhood*,
A heartbreaker, a quiet piece
Not too much like most childhoods
I've seen over my twenty-nine years
Come to think of it, but that's Schumann
And German High Romanticism for you.
Still, how seductive the turns and falls
Of this dream song, especially today
When they seem the one refuge
In a neighborhood of Arab markets
In a city on heightened alert
For bombings at the embassies

And televisions half-gleefully
Report the sorties and reprisals
To reprisals much more like childhood
Than any of this music—
But let the poet go on speaking.
Let's hear everything he doesn't have
To say that will console his people
While in the background rise and fall
The rattlings of the Metro tracks
Like the rhythms of the surf.

## Evensong

Another whistle, another "Joto!"
or "Faggot!" I really shouldn't walk
so much—it endangers my health—
neither should I stay home: the neighbors
saw me kissing my date good night
and they've made up a song about it.

It goes "Honk," "beep," basketball
bouncing high outside my windows, slamming doors
when I go in or out. (There's never
music for this song, may God be thanked.)
The shouts, true to type, come mainly
from pickup trucks and vans that drive off
quickly: they are cowards! *Que dieu soit loué*.
Once, a pickup shouted at my straight brother
and me as we emerged from a liquor/
grocery on Russian Hill: tourists, I'll bet.

I forgot to mention the whistles.
A smidgen of hope remains.
*The Lord is kind and merciful,*
We used to sing at outdoor guitar mass—
We even half believed it. *The Lord is kind*.

## Locked Away

Early seventies: summer afternoons
at swimming pools and long rides home.
The music is very catchy, very bad—
Hamilton, Joe, Frank, and Reynolds'
"Don't Pull Your Love out on Me Baby,"
"Brandy," by Through the Looking Glass,
or "Family of Man," by Three Dog Night.
My brother-in-law is driving; sometimes
he lets us drive. He is morally
far too lax for my parents' tastes;
my first real drunk will be his doing.
At home, the air-conditioners
make a delicious aural womb; they mute
my father's carping, querulous voice.
I sleep and dream I'm in a cage,
lying next to a beautiful father.

The other night, in bed with Leonardo
I saw he was the man half...seen
and half-created in that puerile dream.
But when we had quelled our agitation
we began to talk, we dressed, we walked.
Heaven yawned as before.
Keith Richards sang "I Oughtta Be Locked Away."

I will never make a home
unless it be a palace and a prison,
a spare theme with serious variations.
Only good fathers may live in it
and they are each other's children.
Who are they? How many years away?

CHRYSS YOST

**Chryss Yost** (*Mouth & Fruit*, 2014) is co-editor of Gunpowder Press. She served as Poet Laureate of Santa Barbara from 2013-15; Gunpowder was born during this time. In addition to producing Gunpowder books, she has been a key part of the Shoreline Voices Series. A native of San Diego, she has lived in Santa Barbara since 1990, where she has been a poetic collaborator and organizer for many years with her husband, poet George Yatchisin. She is a SCAD heart attack survivor.

# Childhood

Always a pool by the time we move out,
and weeks to splosh in a red clay pit
while workers curve rebar to fit. We put
on our bathing suits, bright pink and frilled,
and leap into the mud. We mug for the
camera, splay our redded palms, stick out
tongues. We make mud pies, mud roads,
mud houses before they line the shell
with sky-white cement, turquoise tiles at the lip.
It takes days to fill it with the garden hose.
Then we swim. Then we move.

## Echocardiogram

They monitor my etch-a-sketchey pulse.
My heart, a gray fist on the screen,
still inside my body. Thump thump.
Thump thump. There I am. And when
the image freezes, am I there too?
Gasping, ending, screen heart stopped?
A bigger shock not to see you there,
where I was sure you had carved
a home, where I feel you most.

## The Flow

When the water comes, it brings the mountain
and sings the story of the shifting ridge,
summons green to bloom along its edge.
Shapes the hills with patient excavation.

Water comes and carries what we were:
wind-torn leaves, the old path washed away,
the swallowed reflections of hunter and prey.
Brings ash and remains of the bear flag bear.

When water comes, thirst rises for reunion
with the river. All are sullied by the journey.
What blessing to reclaim our purity,
leave the salty stories for the ocean.

We are renewed, to wonder which came first:
that flow of water or this endless thirst?

# Pruning

The plum gnarls its way through
the fall, bark splitting out resin
when the days get honeyed
with late heat. It will die this way,
slowly if we let it, rivered
by beetles and blight.
The rough, sick topography
when we finally get the saw,
tired of the wet plum rot.
The weather of each day
mapped into the branches
stacked to dry on the hearth,
logs that sing in winter's fires,
songs of sweetness and fruit.

BARRY SPACKS

**Barry Spacks** was born in Philadelphia in 1931. He taught at MIT from 1960 to 1981 then at the University of California, Santa Barbara, for 32 years. He served as Poet Laureate of Santa Barbara from 2005 to 2007. A recipient of the St. Botolph's Arts Award, he published eleven poetry collections during his lifetime, including *Spacks Street: New and Selected Poems* (Johns Hopkins University Press, 1982), which won the Commonwealth Club of California's Poetry Medal. An accomplished fiction writer, librettist, singer-songwriter, and actor, Barry Spacks died in Santa Barbara in 2014 at the age of 82.

## Whitewater Vision

Like everyone else I've served my days
lying under the weight of a mountain
breathing stones ... yet always my blood,
like leveling water, knows where it's wanted.

*

Once I had a whitewater vision:
beneath the rage of the rapids I sensed
the undersound of the river's sound ...
indistinguishable from silence.

*

Who am I? Not a solving ... a seeing.
I'd view the storm through eyes of calm.
I'd speak to say
where the silence is.

*

On days when it seems the food for the journey
is clay, not bread, and the spirit famished,
as dusk transfigures everything
I pause, near silence: listening.

## Old Dogs

This old dog
can still bugle and hunt
but the game sees him drowsing
in the corner of the yard
and won't run.

\*

Retriever Heidi, 19,
in her favorite spot on the lawn,
sad eyes wondering
what in hell is going on.

\*

Old Dog, why bother
learning new tricks?
better to teach young tricksters
the old ones.

\*

Young dogs frisk in innocence,
mid-life dogs coarsen, they do, admit it,

but yet arrives, in some long-enduring dogs,
a sort of elegance, a kindliness
that in its way is innocence again.

A knowing child's-play.

*

Old dogs have wisdom,
they realize it makes not a jot or tittle of sense
to retrieve the thrown stick

yet of course they fetch it anyway,
out of compassion, to not make fools
of their grinning young masters.

*

They claim now that dogs can sniff out cancer.
At such work, old dogs must do best.

*

His self-declared new name: "Old Dog" –
fond of pups, nose strong as ever,
a bit slow on the hunt,
but still gives great wag.

# What Breathes Us

Regards to the day, the great long day
that can't be hoarded, good or ill.

What breathes us likely means us well.


We rise up from an earthly root
to seek the blossom of the heart.

What breathes us likely means us well.


We are a voice impelled to tell
where the joining of sound and silence is.

We are the tides, and their witnesses.

What breathes us likely means us well.

JIM PETERSON

**Jim Peterson** has published eight poetry collections, including *Original Face* (Gunpowder Press, 2015), as well as a novel, and a short story collection. He has won The Benjamin Saltman Award for poetry from Red Hen Press, a poetry fellowship from the Virginia Arts Commission, and an Academy of American Poets award. His plays have been produced in regional and college theaters. He retired from Randolph College in 2013 and also taught for many years in the University of Nebraska-Omaha Low-Residency MFA Program in Creative Writing. He lives and writes in the beautiful and mysterious foothills of Virginia.

## Other Laws for the People

We have found the elephant in her lair,
the great white crater-lake beyond her
gouged out by some ancient asteroid
or by the monumental tooth of a glacier.
Is the strangeness of this place a sign

of sacredness? or just an indication
of the loneliness of the beast? The slope
of her forehead, the ascent of her back,
the precipitous troughs and channels
of her flanks, haunches and legs—all suggest

the complexities of a primal epoch,
the immensities of unexplored tundra.
My three colleagues and I take our stand
together. One of us presents her with
a tall book: our proclamations,

our desire to be confirmed in our explanations
of the hand and the fingernail, the face,
the warp and woof of the sky, the necklaces
of words wrapped around our hearts
and throats, the texture of a wing feather,

the universe in a drop of sacrificial blood.
She tilts her head, the grey gates of her ears
swinging on their hinges. One of us
holds out a band of cloth strung
with bells, reverberation among

the wind-scoured walls and towers,
a banishment of silence. She blinks,
lets go a mammoth chuff of breath.
Jingling does not charm her.
One of us spreads his arms in prayer,

casting hopeful side-long glances her way,
imploring her for forgiveness, though
our clarity about sin flew with the last
flocks of southbound starlings and juncos.
She curls her trunk as if speaking to herself,

the white mouth at the end open wide
in small guffaw. I turn my face to the sky
and sing, praising the muscularity
of her thighs, the darkness of her underbelly,
the delicate enormity of her extended tail.

The customary authority of my voice shatters,
shards scrambling like scorpions into gullies.
A small white face peers from the convoluted
warren of her ear, its speech too soft for us to hear.
She uproots one foot and takes an enormous step

closer, continental drift, and the four of us
draw together to make our last stand.
Curious, she only wants to study our text,
perfected scrawl, like the scratches
on stone or tree-trunk she makes with her behind.

## Intersection

I scratch an old tick bite on my left shoulder.
The trail meanders among tall skinny pines

and over fallen trunks. I pick up a stick
and whip the air before my face to scare away

the biting flies. A year ago right here a scream
made me hunker near the ground. Twenty yards

farther on I found the writhing deer, blood
staining her flank around the arrow buried

in her flesh, hooves kicking up the dry
needles, decomposing leaves. Here too, once,

she put her arms around my waist and pressed
her breasts against my back, whispered in my ear

*let's build a fire*. We lay down on our spread jackets,
listened to the wild laughter of the pileated woodpecker

at the intersection of these two trails where
almost no one ever walks but us. Her fingers

traced the fresh stitches on my thigh. A man wearing
camouflage appeared beside the deer, pistol

drawn against her temple. He shifted his tobacco knob
from one cheek to the other, and pulled the trigger.

No News

I like the tight cylinder of a newspaper
and keep it intact, maneuvering the rubber
band to read a line. I'm pulled into the curved
space of a photograph where imagination
completes the scene and the caption.

My methods save me time and a lot of pain.
I don't let myself think about much
except that smoldering potion I'm preparing
for you, complete with chocolate ice cream
on the side and watermelon waiting in the fridge.

See, the phone has lapsed and the street
disappears. I ought to go back to bagging
groceries, which is a study of hands.
Or maybe pizza delivery, where the brain
becomes a map sprouting avenues.

That could be the way to rediscover the way
back to you, since the potion misting my window
has done nothing but bore the birds. Soon I'll
be sliding into some immovable posture,
having drunk the potion myself. I can't

invite you back to this place. My neighbor's
dogs bark too loud at everything that moves.
Only the trees hold time and space together.
The tabby you didn't take with you keeps
landing on the outer sill and squinting in.

Catherine Abbey Hodges

**Catherine Abbey Hodges** is the 2015 winner of the Barry Spacks Poetry Prize from Gunpowder Press for her book *Instead of Sadness* and the author of three other full-length collections: *Empty Me Full* (Gunpowder Press, 2024), *In a Rind of Light* and *Raft of Days* (Gunpowder Press, 2017). Recent poems appear or are forthcoming in such venues as *Narrative, Plume, SALT, RockPaperPoem, Tar River Poetry*, and *CALYX*. English Professor Emeritus at Porterville College, Catherine writes, edits, teaches privately and collaborates with musician Rob Hodges on ancestral Yokuts land.

## Ash Wednesday Morning

The fat candle in the kitchen window burns down
like a rose spilling open. We light a scrap of paper
from the flame, and with the ashes, a little olive oil,
cross each other's foreheads. Margo's in the hospital
again. I stop to see her on my way to school,
go straight from there to class. My students have come
from their night shifts at the nursing home
and Wal-Mart, from Mass, from dropping off the baby
at daycare. They shuffle pages, share staplers.
We look into each other's faces as they hand me their essays.
Who knows how long we've got inside these dusty skins.
We're burning down together, ashes mingling already.

## Thrift

I'd turned to toss my mother's
Braemar sweater, still the deep gold
of turmeric darkening in a skillet but gone
moth-lacy, into the Goodwill bag.

At the last minute I stopped, grabbed
scissors, snipped off the buttons:
mother-of-pearl from a time
of train travel and reel-to-reel.

I poured them hand to hand,
heard them click against each other
like pebbles at the edge of an incoming
tide. Hand to hand to hand.

When we were small, my sister
would shake our mother's bracelet case
when she was gone and imagine her
near—she told me this not long ago—

just out of view, opening the hall closet
or descending the stairs,
bangles sounding.

## Old Blue Shirt

A time zone away, someone I love
is taking a test. For him, I've tried
to hold myself still for a square inch
of time. It's the least I can do
and the most, something like prayer,
but less wordy. This is the boy who saw
an angel down a dim hallway at dawn.
Years later, another in the Grand
Canyon: mineral visitor, feathered flood
and flame. Something passed between
them, I think, though I didn't want to pry.
I haven't seen an angel, but I've taken
years of tests, lately of my vision,
my platelets, my capacity for stillness.
Oh wait a minute. Could the bird
that sang *sweetie sweetie sweetie*
a moment ago really be singing *stupid*
*stupid stupid* now to the same tune?
In my mind a table. On it, the usual
mess, sweet and stupid, stupid and sweet,
and me in my old blue shirt, in a chair
from a long-gone kitchen, looking
out the window at myself looking in,
and both of us thinking: how did we
get here? And can we stay forever?

## By Which I Mean Repent

At my feet, on a plant we call
a weed, the star-shaped husks
of five small flowers form
a new constellation, named
by nobody. Oh friends,

what if we dropped to our knees
before what's hidden, overlooked?
Acacia pods, for instance. Pebbles
on their long, specific ways
toward sand. Ants about their

herculean errands. What if we
praised all that has escaped
our naming, composed hymns
to the limits of our sovereignty,
gathered to sing them? We could

listen to the tongues of the small
of the earth, revise our ways,
by which I mean, you understand,
repent. We could. That sound
like dry leaves lifted by a breeze,

then set down rearranged? I'm
thinking: what if that sound
is salvation rustling in the field
where our dominion ends
and everything else begins.

KURT OLSSON

**Kurt Olsson** was awarded the Spacks Prize for Burning Down Disneyland (Gunpowder Press, 2017). He grew up in Troy, New York and served in the Peace Corps prior to two decades in international development. A longtime Maryland resident, in 2023 he moved to Wisconsin, where he advocates on behalf of mental health and animal welfare. Olsson has two other collections of poetry: *What Kills What Kills Us* and the forthcoming *The Unnumbered Anniversaries*. Olsson's poems have appeared in *Poetry, The New Republic, The Threepenny Review,* and elsewhere.

## Just Once

Come on, who wouldn't just once
like to be the bug-eyed alien with the badass ray gun?
How strange and wonderful
our world would seem
through purple-shuttered lenses. The bizarre sacks
of meat crumpling their soft faceplates,
leaking fuel.
How delicious to say,
*I mean you no harm*
and not mean a damned bit of it.
*Hang in there. Help's coming,* you'd riff
as you coolly flick the safety off
and flip the switch to FRAG
with the most beautiful tentacle in the universe.

# Gold

You want to buy gold, all you can,
which isn't much,

still you'd feel no better. Too much
wrong in the universe today.

Remember the last time
you were happy, really happy.

Lying on your belly before a window
overlooking the bay,

you could see smoke spiraling and twisting up
in the sky. Something big

burning. You didn't need sirens
to know help was coming.

## All God's Creatures

About the flies no one speaks:
the muzzy mass descending onto

Christ's face and hair, mouth and sex,
his delicious wounds.

Nor that the flies sipped oblivion
from his lips, his eyeballs,

then zithered away, warm in their insubstantial
share of him.

The dusk must have shimmered sweeter.
The unruly unknown

tugging them down to earth, for a time,
a trifle weaker.

## The Stars Are Too Far to Need Faces

I am writing this poem to you on Monday.
I will bring it to the post office and mail it.
And then a truck will come pick it up
and bring it to a different truck and this
truck will deliver it to the post office where
you live, and then a postman will drive it
to your mailbox and you will find
this poem, and it will be Wednesday
or Thursday. Which will mean it will be
only a few more days before I see you
again because I will fly on Saturday while
you are in your art class. Maybe while
you're in your art class you can think of
me, and you can draw an airplane and
in one of the windows you can crayon me,
and I will be waving at you and smiling.
Make the day sunny, with just a cloud
or two, and if there are any birds, make sure
they're small birds and not too hungry.

NAN COHEN

**Nan Cohen's** book *Unfinished City* was the inaugural winner of the Dryden-Vreeland Award of Gunpowder Press and a finalist for the Koret Award for an Emerging Writer on Jewish Themes. Her other books are *Rope Bridge* and a chapbook, *Thousand-Year-Old Words*. Her awards include fellowships from the Bread Loaf Writers' Conference and the Yetzirah Conference for Jewish Poets, a Wallace Stegner Fellowship, a Rona Jaffe Writer's Award, and a Literature Fellowship in Poetry from the National Endowment for the Arts. She lives in Los Angeles and serves as the co-director of poetry programs for the Napa Valley Writers' Conference.

# Envy

It twins itself
with a matching
volume of shame,

as inside a new shoe
a proud foot blooms in blisters.

There, in Decembers of the mind,
walking, as it seems, on wounds,

and seeing—perching in one of
its empty trees—a cardinal,

I have envied it the round black eye
that spills a shield of shadow on its throat;
been jealous even of the red

that all about its breast and shoulder
rewards, rewards the bird.

## Ordeals by Water

Before some great change, always as it was in the beginning,
*with a darkness over the surface of the deep*
*and a wind from God sweeping over the water—*

before some great change, the darkness is doubled,
night hovers over, mystery swims beneath.
Outside the body, particles of dusk soften the air;

the eyes see night coming on, the pupil dilates one millimeter
independent of thought or intention.

Inside the body, another body.
With a sudden lunge it has turned and thrust out its feet.
The amnion bulges gently, a bag of waters.

They came there drop by drop.
The body directed some of its waters there
and one day they rose and lifted like a tide.

Without intent, without volition.
A great change going on so slowly,
in the darkness within, in the darkness without.

Can a person change
so the good water will turn
bitter in her mouth?

Can she drink the bitter water,
make it sweet?

## Unfinished City

Passing the house where you once lived, I found
no change I could discern, and so I mourned.
Had something changed, I'd have mourned that too.

But why should bricks and mortar, plumbing, plaster,
laths, electrical wiring have such permanence
when you've left no memento of your presence,
which in its time was solid and complete?

Complete and solid in me lies your absence
since that wretched day when language broke apart
and what I spoke was sensible to me
and what you spoke was sensible to you

but neither understood the other's speech.
Lovingly I took your words into my mouth,
but they were foreign. I had to spit them out.

# Ha'azinu

*guarded him as the pupil of His eye*

Deuteronomy 32:10

Had we known we were safe,
had known we were safe all along...

...as when one comes to the end of a journey
forgetting all the dangers on the way...

...greeting with almost equal delight
the growing and the breaking of the city...

Had we known that the darkness enclosing us
was the same round darkness in the center of an eye...

Had we known, we would have—
but then again, no. And yet,

it is possible to say of each life:
yes, I had one, just like you.

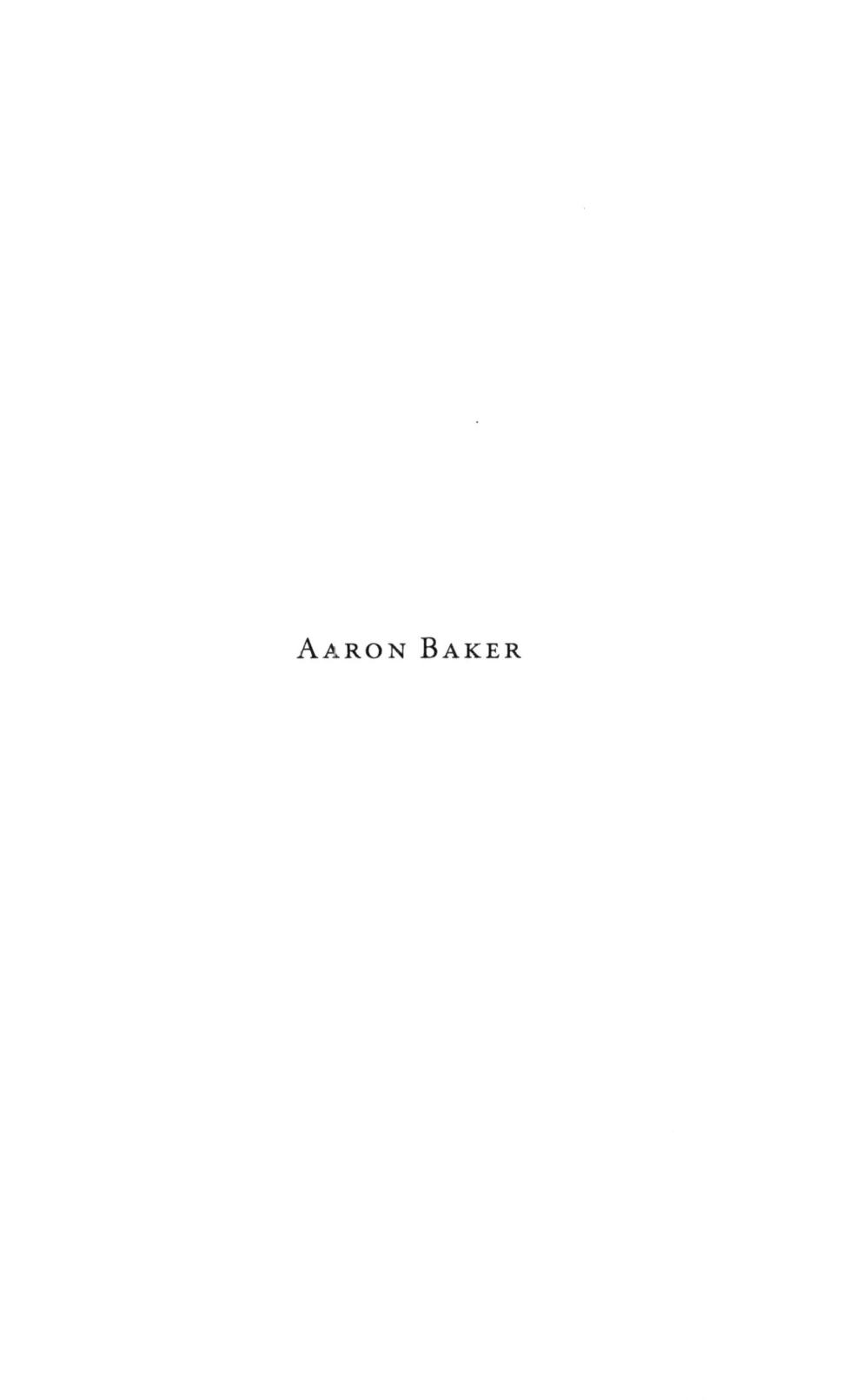

AARON BAKER

**Aaron Baker** is the author of three collections of poetry: *Mission Work* (Houghton-Mifflin), *Posthumous Noon* (Gunpowder Press), and a book-length poem, *American Experiment* (forthcoming from Texas Review Press in Spring 2026). He divides his time between Tucson and Chicago and directs the Creative Writing Program at Loyola University Chicago.

## The Unnaming of the Animals

Now we will unname the animals, now pry from our speech
the syllables that have kept them from the garden.

I cannot say what moves there, the quick tongue flicking
over the fangs, the green eyes aglow in the underbrush,
the hush that falls over the forest as the predator arrives.

Because silence means danger, something might yet survive,
might yet feed in the garden. Now we will unname the animals,

return to the impulse one remove from original sin.
I do not mean original error or mean to say some name
of god that might draw a word nearer to its incarnation.

To name a thing is to claim it, the silver splash in the water,
the cry in the alley, the wing angling into the wind.

To so much as cast out a devil, you must call it by name.
The hiss, the fur beneath your hand, the tail curled
along the back of a sleeping body—let us begin now

to unname the animals! Our father calls out in the garden.
No one answers and he must think us ashamed in our nakedness,

but now we are naked even of our names. Now we release
the animals from our dominion. Let the sheet enfold
and return them to the sky—the stamping hoof, the slashing

claw, the grunt and the feather. We must release them,
release them all that we might unfix and fall out of time.

## The Infernal Regions

Relax. No more the thinness of ceremony.
Largemouth bass at the bottom of Kapowsin Lake
grow still as his thoughts. No swish and silt,

no father and flail. And once perfectly still, they grow
even stiller. Nothing's wasted, says the Lord of the Underworld.
Stillness is economy, and economy exchange.
While he could still speak, my father asked,
"How should I pray for you?"

The curled buds of the bracken fern form
a forest of question marks.

_____

The backhoe operator shuts it down, raises two fingers
towards me and walks off in the rain. Dad's settled
in for the ride, easy now in his pressed suit

and polished shoes. Heavy drops dimple
the freshly-turned dirt. Rainbows of oil in the puddles.
What's left is centuries of silence, such perfect repose.
And potato-salad back at the pot-luck.

_____

Should we look for Orpheus among the living?
Should we look for Orpheus among the dead?

*Father of riches*. Seed the soil, smelt the ore.
We've put on our work boots. We've crossed into
mythology, crossed over. In the underworld,
grief is poor currency. Beneath the camas prairies,

the second-growth Douglas Fir and three bodies
of water, an Atlas of darkness shoulders a weightless

world of light. In the underworld, grief is the only
currency, and music after prayers.
Said Archimedes, "With a long-enough lever
and a place to stand, I will move the earth."

## Dark Matter

We say the heart is sick, meaning something else.
But when we say the body is broken, and it is, the poem,
like a great engine long given up to the weather,
begins to move. Outside, fireweed among the ruins.
We've known the seed of failure in action,
how the worm turns on the root, the foredetermined
uncoiling of the double arms into an electric fizz
and last black sputter of cosmic flatulence. Dark matter:
you take the air, I kick the walls, answer the accusations
to an empty room, then sit down to sob amidst the bones.
It starts to rain. You're elsewhere. *Curse god
and die.* We grow artful when evil, and broken, take
on the utmost of our powers. The garden withers
with such August, but its energy flows inward and flowers.

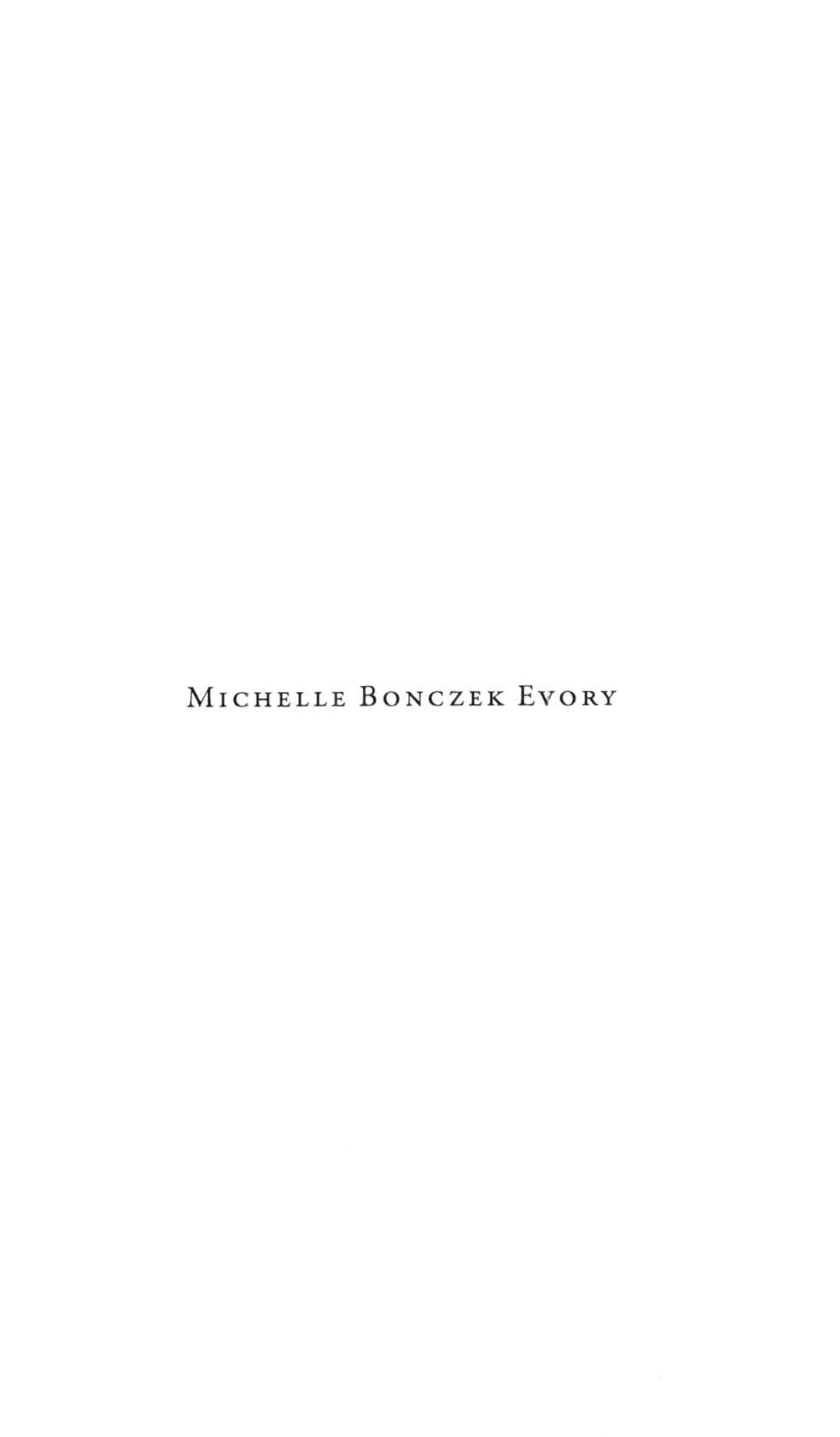

MICHELLE BONCZEK EVORY

**Michelle Bonczek Evory**'s *The Ghosts of Lost Animals* was selected by Lee Herrick as winner of the Barry Spacks Poetry Prize. She is also the author of *The Art of the Nipple, Before Fort Clatsop, A Roadside Attempt at Attraction*, and *Naming the Unnamable: An Approach to Poetry for New Generations*. She is a Visiting Professor of Writing at Oregon Tech and mentors poets at The Poets Billow, an organization founded by her and husband Robert Evory in 2012. She also teaches writing workshops with The Debt Collective fighting to eliminate student loan debt for Americans over 50.

## Yaquina Bay, and Darkness

We have never been down this road: the ocean
a womb, if you can imagine that, and if you can't, just the ocean
pounding a March night black and blue, the lighthouse

at the end of the bay's arm beaming, ready,
metaphorically speaking, for delivery of
what we call the body

from what we call
the body—what we'll call here *our bodies*
from *our life together*—white glare, loose stone,
        the ocean—we fall into it all
blindly, everything—each word

that breaks free from our mouths, each word, that is, that breaks
our mouths, whether right or wrong, for richer or for poorer, each word
forming and forming and forming.

I fear this Pacific rising toward our feet and cringe at the sound
of the horn breaking night
with its wail, this night breaking us.

Every two minutes the horn calls the lost ashore, which feels like me,

which is surely us, out here
lost among tufts of beach grass like wild hair
over the world in which we've lost

the piece of driftwood we used to mark our path
back. Once, I halted, stilled my lungs
for the whisper I heard over my heart. I followed
the sound, sleeplessly, for days. So now

you know it's not good when I say let's stop
walking, let's sit on this log
in this fog, I could say, for as long as it takes to lift,

until the waves stop throwing themselves
against what we cannot see, that which we refuse

to see. I know I don't want to go any further.

Even Niagara Falls sounds like a sigh
from far enough away.

I don't want to go any further, I say.

You close your mouth—no, you, close your mouth, catch
whatever is left of us

not yet lost to this language.

## Leaving South Dakota

You are the lover who leans against the wall
between how it is and how it *is*,

you go to a strip club and spend
a year's worth of love

on flowers that darken
your lap

like our photographs, transformed
from silk and skin into something akin

to teeth marks on a windowsill, a bad habit
craving a complete breakdown.

The Badlands. The first time
you couldn't get it up.

I mean, we'd drunk six beers apiece
and run the Mazda up the muddy-rutted road,

its dirty sides steep, its middle high,
the car skidding and bottoming out—I'd never

felt so alive as on Sheep Mountain Table,
us rolling naked on a vacant hill,

the silent jags
ripped open, sunned and lightning-struck.

The mud-licked tires stayed mud-licked for months,
gray-clumped crusts falling off the rims

onto Kalamazoo streets for weeks,
long after those pretty western suns set.

I told you then I didn't care for the romance
of roses, preferred the simple

white and yellow of a daisy instead, a face
I could trust fully.

But every time your eyes glazed
like dead wings in winter and your body

rocked like a cradle in the kitchen and you fell
asleep in the light, the whole bedroom stunk

of juniper and lies. Always,
when the air feels like this

and the sky looks like it does, I feel drunk and high
on that hill, my heart a tizzy in love,

my head spinning, the sky setting
all around us red and hazy, the black birds,

whatever they are, circling and calling
from some strange gone world, far and low.

GLENN FREEMAN

**Glenn Freeman** won the Barry Spacks Poetry Prize for *Drinking with O'Hara* (Gunpowder Press, 2020). He has published three additional collections of poetry: *Fading Proofs*, *Keeping the Tigers Behind Us*, and *Traveling Light*. He is also an essayist and has published in journals such as *Trumpeter, Green Humanities, Saw Palm*, and *Streetlight*. He has an MFA in poetry from Vermont College and a Ph.D. in American Literature from the University of Florida. He lives in Mount Vernon, Iowa, where he teaches creative writing at Cornell College.

## On Moving One More Time

Late August begins to fall. Birch leaves swirl
in the neighbors' pool. Dried grass, flowers gone
to seed, sun angled lower on the lawn
each day. The scales begin to tip, the world
still weighted with summer's abundance, but
a stone more on the right and everything
shifts. I'd like to think I don't cling
to the past. I've cleaned the house and shut
it tight. Only two lawn chairs and a cooler
remain, some last seed scattered on the ground.
I'll drink a last beer, watch the birds and be
on my way. It's such an aimless future,
the way we're always leaving as if unbound
to this beautiful world, so weather-worn and shabby.

## Fourteen Notebook Fragments after My Mother's Death

1. Delayed flights. Missed connections. The Dr. has said we may not make it in time. Now the car my brother sent to pick us up has gone to Dulles instead of Reagan. My wife says relax. I say my mother is dying. I can't remember if I was good when her mother died. Death doesn't love democracy.

2. Hours by her bedside. Late at night, early morning, evening. We sit; we wait. In the afternoon, I drift to sleep on the couch. Somewhere in my dreams, I can hear nurses talking, the sterile beeps and blips of monitors in hallways, the fan's constant hum on my mother's flushed face. It seems as if there is no longer any there there. Everything is simply metaphor. For what, I know and do not know.

3. 6 AM. My mother wakes to a crystalline blue October sky. *My favorite time of day* she mutters. I realize I never knew that. *I don't want to see it again.*

4. She had said her goodbyes days before. She had left us. Her body, however, had other plans.

5. 3 AM one night, I leave to get some sleep. At the gate, a fox in the headlights. It stares me down then disappears. I know and do not know what to make of it.

6. Happy hour and my brother and I smuggle a few beers into the room. At the sound of tapping glasses, her brows raise. A slight smile.

7. In warm October light, I twirl a dried milkweed pod and watch the seeds lift into the blue. There is a pond. I know and do not know what to make of it.

8. I stare at shaded walls trying to see the images she sees, a painter watching the light in ways I couldn't comprehend. The irony, I thought, knowing that in my younger days it would have been me seeing things on the walls.

9. Afternoon sunshine beside the stream. Autumn leaves, cattails, and squirrels. In a field of wildflowers gone to seed, I watch a fox hunt then disappear without a sound. I know and do not know what to make of this.

10. *Who is that?* she says with eyes suddenly wide. *Who's behind me?* She says with nothing but a wall behind her. I won't repeat myself.

11. One morning, I leave my father's apartment before daylight to be sure to be in my mom's room when the doctor makes his early morning rounds. I don't know what I wanted to know. Muffin and cup of coffee in hand, I walk out the door as my father's light comes on in his back room and I see him shuffling his slow shuffle, the befuddled sadness of now living alone even while she's alive. I should stop and talk with him, but I can't. God knows what I want to know.

12. I don't know how many times I can repeat myself.

13. The priest tells me my eulogy should be brief. It is, after all, about bringing people into the church, not about my mother. I want to say no. I want to tell him that he's not going to bring me into the church that way. But, then again, what should it matter to any of us.

14. My brother and I confirm the body. I wanted to say no. This was not her. The wrinkles and lines on her face that made her who she was all smoothed down to stone, the life ironed away. This was not her. But I knew they just wanted to confirm they weren't going to cremate someone else's mother. I know, I know. What should it matter to any of us.

# Oh Yeah!

*for Mingus*

If we could strip away the world's logic,
I'm sure we'd find a rhythm like this:
wave on top of wave, preposterous
and perfect, pounding on shore, a music

with its coast ever shifting, around, over, through—
prepositions without context, your voice
lost behind the din of its own chaos.
If we dig to where the rhythm runs true,

we would find your bass line, driving and driven,
swirling and syncopated, and you
buried in the mix, shouting and stuttering, a few
mumbles and groans. Your music will not forgive.

Relentless, it stops wordless in its tracks,
a pool of nouns longing for their syntax.

PEG QUINN

**Peg Quinn's** debut poetry collection, *Mother Lode*, was published by Gunpowder Press in 2021. She has a BFA in Education from the University of Nebraska, Lincoln. Her poetry and non-fiction have been published in numerous journals and anthologies and four times nominated for the Pushcart Prize. She lives in Santa Barbara California where she is an educator and visual artist.

# Commuter's Ode to a Pear Tree in a Thunderstorm

With branches raised
in resplendent surrender, you
welcome the storm's rough touch
on your rain-blacked trunk.

Blissfully ravaged by wind,
your celebration
casts a blesséd mess
of white petals
cloaking the ground below,

transforming this dark morning
at a glance.

# Every Death a Reckoning

*for Jackson Wheeler*

Learning of your passing swept me
into Death's country, where I
do not speak the language,
though the clatter of everyday living
flows past like water around
my solid stone of emptiness.

And the wind, howling through trees
or maybe
trees, crying in the wind.

Doors and windows rattle, and though
I'm of no man-made religion, it is silence
and a clear bell ringing I need.
I long for ritual, like sitting shiva.

You gone.
Everyone in the room but you.

Or, your presence fills the room.

The world transformed,
your absence a vacuum,
your voice silenced.

Or, your voice a steady whisper.

# A Note of Thanks

*Honey, get it while you can.*
*—Janis Joplin*


A well-kept black Buick crept through the parking lot
as if time no longer mattered, eventually found a spot,
and cautiously, came to a stop.

Thank you, elderly man in hip denim jacket and worn
baseball cap, who creaked in slow motion around the back
to the passenger's side to aid a small woman,
her one daring toe touching pavement.

Thank you, stylish high heel with striped sock,
frail and waiting.

Thank you, practiced precision.
With arms gently clutched,
he eased her up.

When steady, she held him with the wide smile of love,
while arranging a too-large sweater.

Oh, thank you, smile and tangled clothes.

He leaned down low, eyes closed.
Even their kiss was long and slow.
Thank you.

## Spring Planting

Let dirt fall endlessly
through your fingers
like you did when
innocent of the world's
complications
Slowly fill your lungs
with earth's rich scent
Plow a furrow curved
to contain the will of water

Marry seeds in ritual pairs,
pushing earth firm
to secure their future

Praise the symphony
of sunlight
listen, part of you
is planted here, too
feel your future taking root
as you walk the splattered shade
of blooming dogwood
back to the rest of your life

MEGHAN DUNN

**Meghan Dunn** is the author of *Curriculum*, winner of the 2020 Barry Spacks Poetry Prize from Gunpowder Press. She lives in Brooklyn, NY, where she teaches high school English. Her work has appeared in *Ploughshares*, *Narrative*, *Poetry Northwest*, *Ecotone*, and *Four Way Review*, among others, and has been featured on *Verse Daily* and *The Slowdown* podcast. She has received scholarships from the Bread Loaf Writers' Conference, the Sewanee Writers' Conference, and the Fine Arts Work Center in Provincetown.

## After a Student's Suicide

Useless anyway, all these thoughts of why,
of what we could have noticed and did not.
Better we should contemplate the sky,

which has no answers, but a blue our eyes
can rest on, comprehend, a simpler knot.
Useless anyway, all these thoughts of why.

Instead, let us consider this day's light,
a brilliance we know cannot be caught.
Better. Let us contemplate the sky,

the sun in its clear and limited supply,
the shadows it designs, the expected night.
Useless anyway, all these thoughts: why,

what we could have noticed, a cracked gaze,
a leaving glance, an away-ness in her throat.
No. Better we should contemplate the sky.

Not the child with her serious smile,
her shy light, her meticulous thought...
Useless anyway, all these thoughts of why.
Better we should contemplate the sky.

# Because I Fainted During the Miracle of Life Video in Seventh Grade

I never saw the birth and no one would describe it to me
when I emerged from the nurse's office, the other girls

giggling knowingly, their hands to their mouths,
while the ice pack I held pressed to the nape of my neck

melted into the loose ends of my ponytail.
I had to imagine it instead. I pictured a tunnel

the color of my flushed cheeks, the smooth cool
of the linoleum against my face, the murmur

of the class coming into focus around me.
I didn't know where the tunnel went or why,

but I knew it was something miraculous.
Something to change me.

Years later, it was light when I got on the train
and when we emerged from the tunnel, it was dark.

We were on the bridge, high above the river,
the air frozen on the train windows in shattered

circles, my face looking back at me from the glass,
lines around my eyes like little knives. I was old.

My whole life had happened already.
But somewhere in the reflection was the girl

returning to class, the nurse's office pass crumpled
in her damp palm, waiting to be filled in, to learn

what she'll give birth to, not knowing yet it's herself,
over and over again, the pain cresting and falling,

pushing and crying out until she holds herself,
bloodied, in her arms, finally,

the miracle she's been waiting for.

## Historical Context: Two Lesson Plans

1.

My students study the lynching photos,
study the smiles on the faces of onlookers,
the postcards plastered with the images
mailed to relatives with greetings, expressions,
even, of love. The men in the photos, the murderers,
they thought they were saving their women, their children,
from something. They thought they had a good reason
for what they did. I study the faces of my students
studying the photos. I too think I have a good reason.

2.

When showing a documentary, I tell my students
I'll say when to shut their eyes.
Ten minutes in, a girl starts crying.
*You said you'd tell us when to shut our eyes,* she sobs.
On the screen, a man hangs from a tree.
The family below him smiles.
The small boy sits on his father's shoulders,
his blond hair almost brushing
the feet of the hanged man.
My student is still crying.
*Close your eyes,* I say.

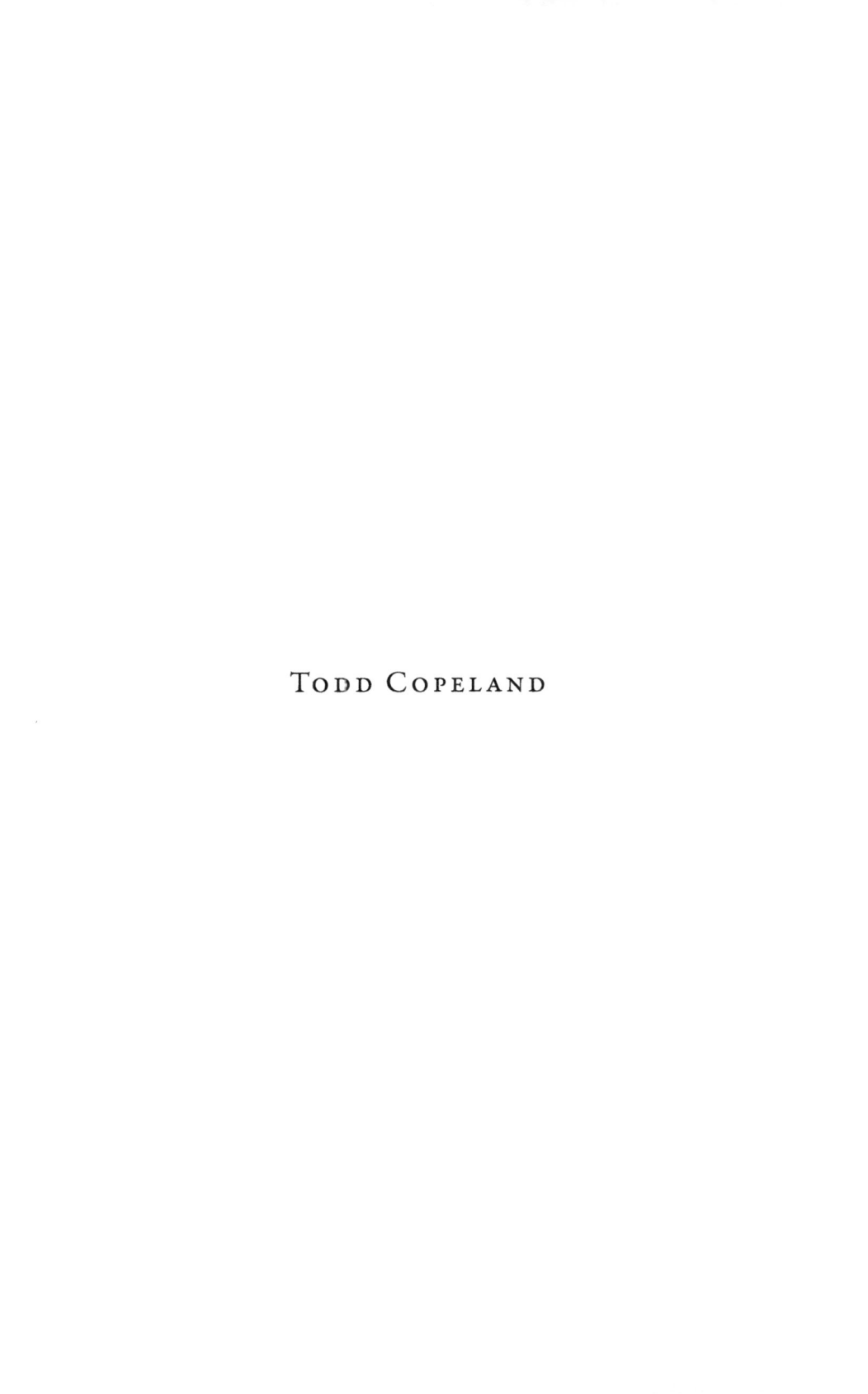

Todd Copeland

**Todd Copeland** lives in Waco, Texas, and is the author of *Like All Light* (2022), winner of the Barry Spacks Poetry Prize from Gunpowder Press. His other works include the narrative nonfiction book *The Immortal Ten* (2025), and his other awards include the John H. Jenkins Research Fellowship in Texas History from the Texas State Historical Association (2025). His poems have appeared in *Image*, *Christianity & Literature*, and *Sugar House Review*, among other publications, and his essays have been published in such journals as *Literary Imagination* and *JNT: Journal of Narrative Theory*.

# The Cast Line

*in memory of William Chad Copeland*

The water has the shine of worked gold
where the low sun replicates itself,
refulgent and oblong, across Aransas Bay.

Forty yards offshore, working a wharf's
barnacled pilings for redfish and trout,
my father and I stand sideways to the glare—

human from the waist up, ocean below.
There's an eroticism to these early hours,
the spuming combers exhausting themselves

in an aubade on the landward slope,
the matutinal wind soft on the back of the neck.
Morning brings back the heroic ages,

Thoreau said, and perhaps he's right.
Beyond Rockport's bait shops
and greasy spoons, past houses on stilts

down the dirt road out of town
where wild grass and oleander border
the shoreline's thin strip of crushed shells,

my father's touched by an air of the fabulous
that suggests it's not so much real life
he lives but some charmed perfection of it.

Slowly, his arm goes back. The rod
ranges the sky. The slender shadow
of his cast line lives on the bright water.

## Jefferson River Road

Sure, we saw him plenty around town,
going into Wuxtry,
browsing the aisles at Jackson Street Books,
always in those cotton dress shirts
bought at Goodwill.

It was 1991, the year punk broke,
but we knew nothing
would ever feel as good
as dancing to side A of *Doolittle*
with that other Todd.

No one suspected the chaos of his heart,
the extremity of his desire.
He was doomed from the start,
we said, for all his careful artistry.

O sweet, feigned innocence.
O newlywed Dionysus
in a small house among the pines.

# Glimpsed

Saint Cuthbert
left the monastery of Lindisfarne
for the kind of blessed solitude we craved,
the blues and whites of his Northumbrian noon
a balm to both mind and soul.

We preferred
picturing him in his last hours,
his bed pulled to a window
in the island hermitage where,
between blocks of roughhewn stone,
cormorants would flash
across an allowance of sky.

The deep shadows of dusk
would have slowly filled his room,
pagan and nonspecific,
the coming night a final darkness
through which waving torches
would signal his life's end
across water to Holy Island.

## Nine Mile Mountain

I leave snowshoe tracks
in a winter's worth of powder
that my son follows for a time

before making his own way
up the mountain. At ten,
alive in this snow-filled Arcadia,

why wouldn't he believe his steps
could be his alone? That our tracks
left behind in the quiet forest

will soon guide our return?
When my father died near Cloudcroft,
the ambulance speeding down

toward the Tularosa Basin,
I followed fifteen minutes behind.
He was always in the lead.

In the hospital, near the body,
his black work boots stood alone
on a countertop as if waiting

for use by the back door at home.
My father will never rest in peace.
I imagine his figure up ahead

moving among the ascendant pines,
his snowy steps waiting for ours
to come to life, to shape oblivion.

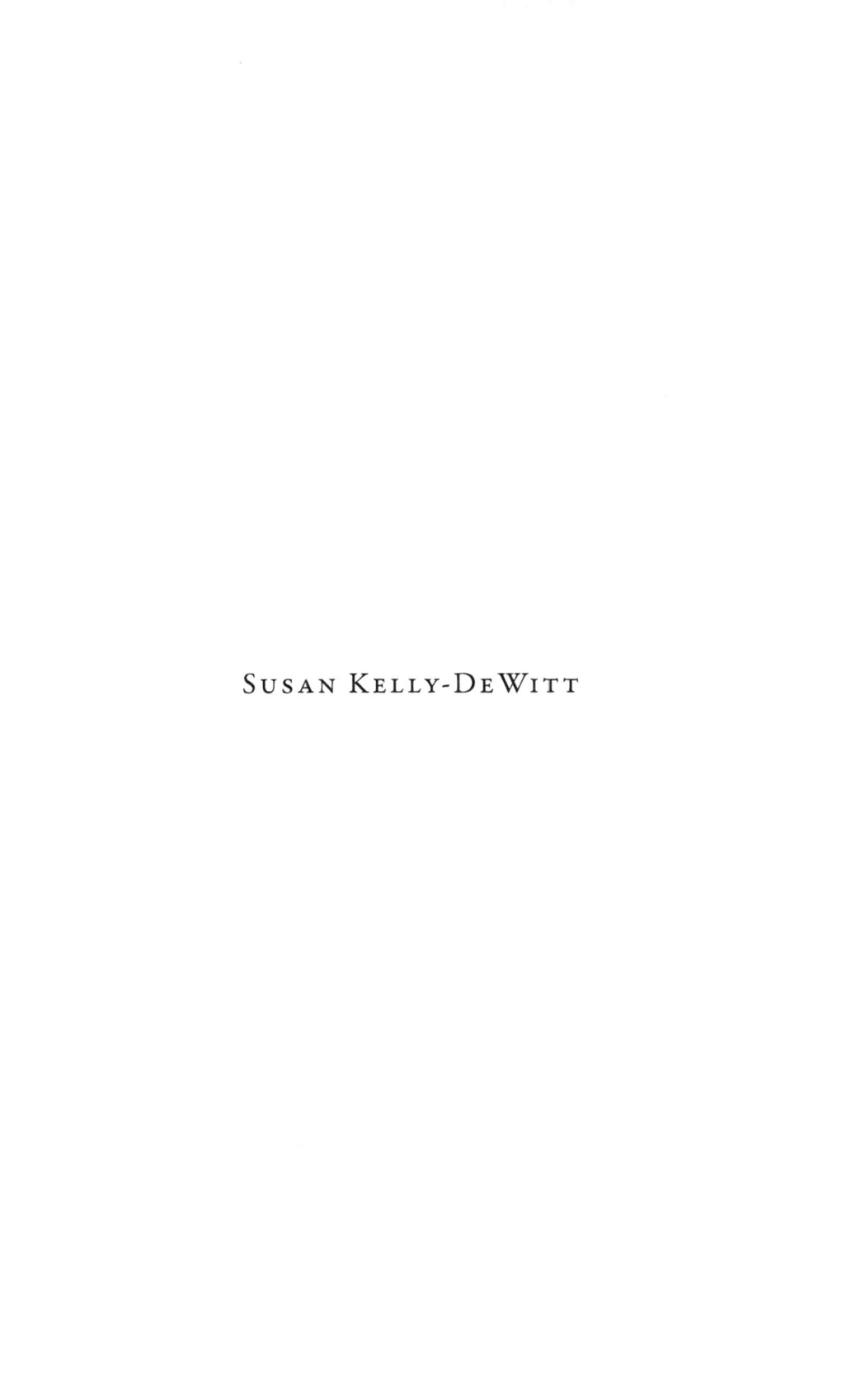

SUSAN KELLY-DEWITT

Narcissus

In January, many gray voices wheedle
*Time to give up...*

The leaves left on the shivering
limbs seem to listen.

The wind makes them tremble
like toothless old men,

to teach us a lesson.

But the paper whites, fresh from sleep,
aroused, want us to love them

more than our despair.
We believe them

when they promise us the stars,
when they whisper sweet

nothings in our ear.

## Calling The Horses

You whistle
and they turn their heads—

A roan mare pushes up slowly
from the dusky pasture grasses;
a palomino and a chestnut bay
follow in sequence behind her—
they move toward us
without conviction. The mare's
belly slumps with the weight
of her unborn foal, as we call to them
across barbed wire.

(In our minds we beg
for the victory of their close looks,
but they stop, refuse to look longer,
turn away the grazing darkness
of their eyes, fall back to each other.)

Wild oats silver the fields, bluebottles
leap up along the roadside
in four fringed colors. I stoop to gather
a few wild panicles—
the crushed juice of the broken
stems perfumes my thumbs.

It feels like beauty,
the way the colors hold
themselves out
to be touched.

## Teaching Poetry in the Prisons

I think of him
as a victim
(a veteran)

of war—
every day was
the enemy

in a house-
hold that thought

children should
be punished
with barbed wire,

belts, burns, punches,
pinches, slaps, kicks,

starvation. Where meth
was the vitamin,
sex was the money,

where poverty was
the neighborhood,

poverty was
the country

and nobody ever
called him honey

until high school
freed him to be

part of something
larger than himself,

a gang. They robbed
a convenience
store; someone got

shot, killed—he did not
pull the trigger yet

here he is twenty
years later, life

without parole—
shaking my hand,
smiling at me,

thanking me
for helping him learn

one new word.

SANDRA MCPHERSON

**Sandra McPherson** is the author of *Speech Crush*, part of the California Poets Series from Gunpowder Press. She published 21 prior collections. She taught for 23 years at the University of California at Davis and 4 years at the Iowa Writers' Workshop. The founder of Swan Scythe Press, she recieved grants and fellowships from the Ingram Merrill Foundation, the Guggenheim Foundation, and the National Endowment for the Arts.

## Current, Matadero Creek

Down there would have been my mother,
under the swags of vines,
wading through flats of light.

Prickly, linty tanoak leaves. Minnowy navigation
maternal eyes could see.
Threatened red-legged pocket frog.

Willow. Stiff bay. A doe caught wet-hoofed
on a camera manned only by night.
Missing mother combing for watercress.

*Time is a river without banks,*
says Chagall. Maybe, she's thinking;
maybe she's thinking...

Mats of peppery greens, stony shallows,
while up on the topsoil pepper pinks the trees—
neither native, both adoptees.

Buson says it another way:
*It doesn't go on from here...*
*The narrow path ends*

*in the water parsley...*
No slovenly, apathetic puddles for us, Motherwater.
I'm specimen of your current. And don't we

get stranger as we let the familiar go?

# After Trauma

All I ever needed to bring up with her was cranberries.
She brightened no one's eyes; I befriended her frown.
*Bogs*, she says, when I rhyme *fog*.
Bone-chilling overcast, she affirms damply.
Wouldn't you like to slip away from your burned house
and head to the cold coast, even if they have to search
for you? I did that when the fire of marriage
scorched my heart. I hid in the low mist.
I was three months along and wanted to lie with the deer.
Mushroomy bottomland, its spires raised in purples and blues,
swamp ferns and skunk weed filled in with frogs.
Ditches soaked clean cattails muddy.
I used to wear a watch: if I wasn't found, I'd turn around.

Ravens flew to the corner of my eye like forests of winged ink.
I knew she felt their cinders too:
Though she was safe here, I saw her rise
out of her wheelchair and swing at the nurse.
An aide held me back. It shook me, but now
my violent friend sounds calmed, discussing cranberries.
Where all do they grow? Why don't we eat them always?
I want us to talk next of blackberries. But no, she says,
blueberries are next; they grow here too
and she can feel their essence, their gist, from long ago.
Blueberries it is; we're on a roll, our moods indigo.

# Speech Crush

...who spoke late
echolalic, then in similes,
by the lake,
where the sticks were her
long mosquitoes, her lava
pyramid brown rice.
 Got a crush on a suffix,
giggled, blushed,
at every *-tion*. And there were
many, in conversation,
flirting with her.
Pre-dejection.
Pseudoabstraction.
 As she grew into
orchestration, a white
sportcoat and a pink
carnation, crenellation,
inhalation—
had I known
too much lamentation?
 I, who have lived
isolation, seen sun
as lion,
its mane's
diffusion; offered her
a turnip moon,
close-shaven.
Parental anomaly,

weird shared ions.
A word-prescription.
A nerve-ending infatuation.
 I'm blessed
she's the termination of me,
last blood relation.
Daughter, if you follow land
to its suffix, there's *ocean*,
which I know your toes,
bare, still-growing, slim,
will never *shun*.

DENNIS SCHMITZ

**Dennis Schmitz**'s posthumous collection, *Our Music* (2022), is part of the Gunpowder Press California Poets Series. He taught at several colleges in the Midwest before coming to California State University, Sacramento, in 1966, where he was a beloved professor of English for over thirty years. His collections include *We Weep for Our Strangeness, Double Exposures, Goodwill, Inc., String, Singing, Eden, About Night, The Truth Squad,* and *Animism.* He was named the first poet laureate of Sacramento in 1994. He died in 2019 at his home in Oakland, California.

## Two-Beer Ethics

Suppose, Tanaka argues, a school-bus—
kids. Behind the bus-glass you see the stew

of heads & sweatered elbows & a necessary
driver in his own square of glass, & give him,

for spite, snowmelt on a county blacktop.
Tanaka by now has the fly trapped inside

his bar glass against which, half-wet, it bats
fumes. Tanaka is Aristotle, he's the Angel

Moroni—he knows I won't argue two-beer
ethics, but he makes the children anyway

& supposes the snow, & out of High Street's
turns he brings the bus to the hypothetical

old woman crossing illegally as the bus
downshifts into Tanaka's icy county road.

To save the children, he says, the driver hits
the old woman—the driver intends to save

the children so it's fine to hit the old woman,
but maybe the driver shouldn't take joy

in hitting her—intention saves the driver
moral dereliction, Tanaka says, & lifts the glass

away from the fly he didn't intend to drink.

## Systems

Any system works at its own suicide
its own way like our scavenged

'36 Packard my dad called *Dowager*,
or a system of endangered but inbred

plover closed off in a few acres
of Point Reyes sand. Or, system within

systems, my Berkeley neighbor planting
his Ford pick-up with nasturtiums—

hood gone, more dirt shoveled in through
the windows, the truck pretend-trucking

a bed-load of lantana & poppies uphill
into our shared driveway. Or, earlier, entropy

in my '70s Wisconsin commune. Never *wrought*
enough to be *over-wrought*, I thought why not

just turn over & dream in this fertile dark?
& why not, at night, tonight, steal one swim

more if the community pond too is a system
& the wind's underbelly dragging through

pond grass is only the story's way
to distract me from drowning?

## The Other Side

The way motel walls are
so thin that you hear

the polyglot of lovers
the exchange of groans

the sleepers turning
over in the cheap beds

the late-night
flushes—there is a thin

wall between being old
& the personal death that's just

on the other side,
but at 78, I instead hear

music from
that other side—

a low thrill, some song—
familiar, more than one voice

when there is a voice,
& I begin to hum too.

## 80ᵀᴴ Birthday

I've already packed extra socks
in case there is an after-life

& let the years do their own math.
I was delivered to my mother

a leaky vessel & loud—
the nurse, I saw, was impressed,

& I was issued a childhood.
Today I re-gift your praises

as I walk in the rain that's shredded
to mist by the eucalyptus.

I praise this break in the never-done
Calif drought that still crackles

underfoot. My $30 gift shirt is wet,
my sandals slide, but I rejoice

in this birth-day of everything around me.

GARY SOTO

**Gary Soto** is the author of the pandemic-inspired *Downtime* (Gunpowder Press, 2021). He was born and raised in Fresno, California, is the author of thirteen poetry collections for adults, most notably *New and Selected Poems*, a finalist for both the Los Angeles Times Award and the National Book Award. His prose titles include *Living Up the Street*, *A Summer Life*, *Jesse*, *Buried Onions*, and *The Effects of Knut Hamsun on a Fresno Boy*. He has written for the stage, including the libretto *Nerdlandia*, the musical *In and Out of Shadows*, and the one-act *The Afterlife*. He is the author of "Oranges," the most anthologized poem in contemporary literature. He lives in Berkeley, California.

## Travel Plans

Won't get to Peru. Bolivia is out of the question.
Siberia? I wouldn't live to tell the grandkids
Of the sand that creeps along the steppes.
Can't say I'll suck on a hookah in Cairo
Or sample grasshoppers in Chiapas.
A toboggan ride in Greenland?
Reindeer meat in Estonia?
I would love to befriend a bunny in the Highlands
And choke down a plate of haggis.
The Taj Mahal is off the radar
As is flyfishing in Mongolia—
Tempting, but no. *Saludos* to Argentina
And Spain, but no to the Azores at twilight,
The sunsets on the water, then not on the water.

I have a grasp on my limitations.
Won't tap a toe to accordion street music in Paris,
Pet a duck in the Cotswolds,
Or retrace my ancestral steps
Up Teotihuacan. Won't bicycle
A country that I can't spell—is it Lechenstein?
Shake the paw of a comrade in Bulgaria? No can do.
Cuba? *Ay, papi,* to ride shotgun in a '55 Chevy,
A convertible of course, my hair loss
More evident when we pick up speed,
The tip of my cigar glowing ruby red.

I'm not much of a traveler,
Though my ambition is to spin
A prayer wheel in Tibet.
And like Philip Larkin, I would love to go to China
If I could get back on the same day.

## Questions Not Asked in Catechism

Who prompted the finch to visit the lawn?
    The cat and the cat's shiniest fang.
Who fed the worm between storms?
    Mother Earth in all her wetness.
Who sent the geese flying south?
    Mother Earth when she was done with the worm.
Who drank from the plate of milk?
    The cat after he finished the devil's long-tailed rat.
Who questioned the angels?
    God did, but He didn't bother to listen.
Who appeared from a leaf fire in the gutter?
    A mystery man who became the Holy Ghost.
Who righted the child after he fell from his bike?
    A stranger, who offered a dollar to make it all right.
Who was that boy?
    Not Jesus or Abraham, not Buddha or Mohamad,
    More a boy who wept with a hand over his eyes.
    His three wounds? All in his heart.

# Talking about the Afterlife

And I said,
I'm taking flying lessons—
You're gonna be my first passenger.

My poet friend said,
Man, I would have a better chance
With a chimp at the controls.

Laughter without drinks,
Laughter with a sober tear in our eyes.

I said, Oh, the chimp's coming along.
He's the co-pilot.

Then we drank,
And talked about the chance
Of life after this life,
At any altitude,
With or without a grinning chimp.

We tapped beers,
Drank, revisited the saga
Of our hair lost on Highway 99.

Pondered old age and adult diapers.
On the propeller job
Altitude five thousand feet and rising...
You never know how long the flight will last.

# I Picture It

My dear wife walks across a vacant lot
Where it's always 1952,
With a blimp in the eastern sky,
Factory noise down the street,
Trucks like hell-bent rhinos,
A single plum tree that flowers in all seasons.

My wife pulls a Ziplock bag
From her purse, opens it,
Looks in, says, Goodbye, Gary, it was pretty fun...
And pours my ashes
Onto the sandy ground
Where I once played, fought,
And made shards of broken bottles
Wink with sunlight—my childhood fun.

She shakes out my remains,
Says a Shinto prayer with eyes mostly closed.
She next glances up at the inverted bowl of polluted sky:
A cigar-shaped blimp, the shreds of clouds.
She turns to the rustle from the knee-high weeds.
Boots, my cat? Has he come to show me the way?

How the sand sucks up tears,
And there are tears.
She prays a Christian prayer just to be sure,
Then shakes the Ziplock bag,
The remaining inch or two
Of human ash directionless in wind,
Faint as a shadow, the stuff of rumor that became fact:
My human soot that didn't fly very far.

CATHERINE ESPOSITO PRESCOTT

**Catherine Esposito Prescott** is the author of *Accidental Garden*, winner of the Barry Spacks Poetry Prize (Gunpowder Press, 2023), and two chapbooks, *The Living Ruin* and *Maria Sings*. Recent poems appear or are forthcoming in *Colorado Review*, *Josephine Quarterly*, *NELLE*, and *Poets Reading the News*. Prescott is the co-founder of SWWIM and editor-in-chief of *SWWIM Every Day*. In addition to her work in poetry, Prescott teaches yoga philosophy and leads yoga and writing retreats.

## Instructions: Our Next Lifetime

When karma brings you back around,
I want you to find me, so we
can travel to southern Spain again.
You won't eat octopus. I won't eat it either,
but we'll feast on all the olives and the flesh
of blood oranges. When you come back,
I want to trace the last vestige of tomato
sauce from your plate, lapping it with crusty bread.
I'll learn the slang of my ancestors next time.
I want to tell you dirty jokes in their native
tongue. When you come back, find me
scattering red rose petals, white jasmine
flowers, and lotus buds in a temple while thinking
your name. Find me on a beach at sunrise.
Find me walking the shore, stepping around broken shells.
Find me racing down a city block. Find
my body moving in the direction of its longing.
Find me plunging into oceans, into rivers,
and lakes. Find my eyes scaling mountains.
Find me whispering to the sacred ficus
tree in my backyard, every word moving
like song up the tree's spine from canopy
to roots. Find me tying gold threads and glass bracelets
around the tree. Find me planted there.
Next time around, press your ear
to the ground. Feel my voice calling you.

## Ode

the flock of wild lime-green parrots
the clusia hedge with fat, waxy leaves
the butterfly bush and porterweed
the milkweed which seems frail but hosts dozens of cocoons
the moon which has now set
the sun as it charges over the beach, turning the world on as it rises
using "it" instead of "she"—giving the feminine a break
the pen that works, the fingers that hold it
the teenage boys who grow their minds at school
the daughter with unicorn dreams
the husband also rising
the quiet morning, then the raucous afternoon
the evening with its petty arguments
the soccer, the climbing, the gymnastics
the beautiful bodies of children
the athletes who challenge gravity, who move beyond the mind's limitations
the mind that tries to sit still
the body that yokes
the genders, the skin colors, the dances, the songs, the languages in which
     the same thoughts are set to new music
the engineers & programmers who abet the artists
the eyes—of course—even as print gets smaller
the senses—interpreting
the chance run-ins, the surprise diagnoses, truths spoken
the healers who radiate compassion
the seekers who find new pathways to understanding
the concept of infinity, which I cannot grasp—
the universe unaware of pushing outward
I imagine my mind without boundaries, my heart without boundaries
a wall becomes mirage, a line something to jump over

infinity on a macro scale and a micro scale
beyond quarks, beyond matter as particles as energy as imperceptible waves,
    what if this unfolds infinitely—
what if the cells travel inward forever
the heart and its cosmos, the brain and its cosmos, keeping your world steady
when you pick up the children from school, cook some spaghetti
the children orbiting you, you orbiting them
the spaces between you, full, collapsed
breathing in their wonder, you exhale yours.

## Accidental Garden

Did we plant a butterfly garden or did monarchs stumble on
the heirloom tomatoes that need pollen to transfer from pistil to stamen?
Big job, poor job to pollinate plants, without anthem, without a
bang, without music, an inaudible buzz. Flippant-seeming flutterers
have made this garden more than a green riot. I don't know an insect's
intention, but today we have bulbs of chocolate striped tomatoes, fistfuls
　　　of cherry
or grape tomatoes. I cannot remember which we planted; the forgotten
are numerous, are prolific, names of species, of genera. Sages say that
we all have consciousness—me, as the one who writes this—but also
a butterfly, a green parrot, an ant, a bee, our cat, and every tomato plant.
　　　Who is
divine? All of us scattered together on this earth like thrown dice—all
accident, all planned—with little more to do than to touch one thing,
　　　transform another.

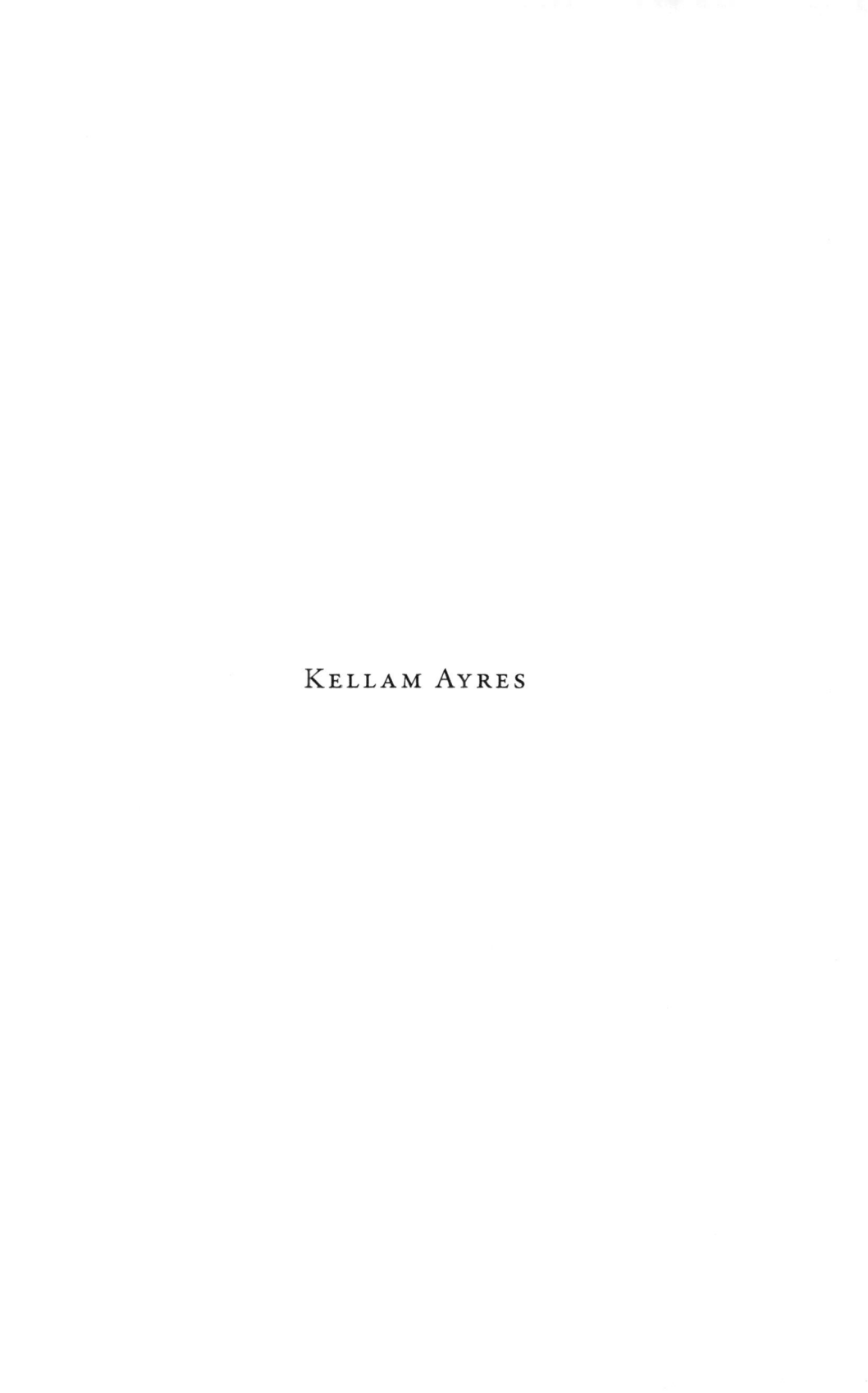

KELLAM AYRES

**Kellam Ayres's** debut poetry collection, *In the Cathedral of My Undoing*, was the winner of the Barry Spacks Poetry Prize and was a finalist for the 2024 New England Book Awards. Her poems have appeared in *Ploughshares, New England Review, Ninth Letter*, and elsewhere. She works for the Middlebury College Library and lives with her family in Vermont.

## Summer

A young woman was pleasuring herself
on a pine tree that had fallen across
the narrow river where I went to fish,
straddling the trunk, her feet just breaking
the water, her body leaning forward
with hands pressed into the bark.
White shorts rode up her thighs and bunched
at her crotch as she settled into an uneven rhythm.

I thought of love, and you, my love.
But here, now, I see it—watching her ride the tree,
lifting one hand and then the other to wave
at the sky like a conductor, this quiet expression of pleasure,
this face of surprise. Strange angel—
no matter how much she rocked herself
she would not loosen the tree from its resting place,
she would not set forth down the river,
drifting somewhere new, somewhere east of here.

Snakes

Should I start with their names?
Roscoe, Willy, Big Tom, Mr. No Shoulders.
Of course I hated them,

their special tanks and lamps,
the feeding ritual. Those tongues.
The way I never felt safe.

And their sad habitat—
plastic rocks and sticks, plastic caves.
It wasn't their fault, but he—

he was the worst. One afternoon
while I was at work he took everything,
mine and his, but left his four snakes

in aquariums in the living room,
where my mother's antique table had been.
He used to pick up the snakes

and they'd wrap around his forearm.
He'd get off on it, the tightening
and squeezing, thrusting them in my face

because he knew what it did to me.
In their tanks they'd slide
over a thick piece of fake driftwood,

their scales shimmering under the heat lamp.
White mice were living in a cardboard box.
The frozen, pre-killed prey were stacked

in the freezer.
I knew how to keep everyone alive.
Did what I needed to do.

I sacrificed the mice to the snakes' hunger,
sold the snakes to a guy down the road,
and moved to a new place.

But does it make for a better story
to keep one mouse alive? To name him
Lucky, and for Lucky and me to live together?

## The Haunting

In our village, the night sky flashes
with light, a storm of cloud, and at home,
phone sex between neighbors.
They text one-handed, their silent mouths
open and close to suggest longing,
or agony, or disbelief. Pleasure,
they've learned, has many masks.

Outside, a harvester fires up before dawn.
A tractor stands ready to spread manure.
What the woman said about her body,
what the man said is so hard—
words have taken them beyond the boundaries
of home, beyond the children and orchard
and greenhouse, the hen house—
an astonishing, impermanent relief—
words rising above the sweet loam,
the damp earth bathed in shit, crossed endlessly
by backhoe and mower, milk truck and draft horse.
Teenagers with buckets of feed before school,
texting too, to their friends, before hopping the bus.

We think they are still beautiful, our young,
we're convinced their virtue
does not dissolve each day—
but they've studied us, and so, already,
are caught by an ache that will linger for years.
And we think how hard it is to sustain this land,
this living, to keep on living—
how closely we toe ruin each day.

CHRISTOPHER BLACKMAN

**Christopher Blackman** is a poet from Columbus, Ohio. His poems have appeared in *The Kenyon Review*, *DIAGRAM*, *Cleaver Magazine*, *Southeast Review, Booth, and Epiphany*, among other publications. Former co-host of the podcast *Poem Party*, he received his MFA from Columbia University, and has been an instructor for the Kenyon Review Young Writers' Workshop. He was a finalist for the National Poetry Series, and a semi-finalist for the Autumn House Press Poetry Prize. He currently lives outside of Boston and works at Dana Hall School, a 5-12 Day and Boarding Girls School in Wellesley, Massachusetts.

## The End of the Party

Is anything sadder
than the clearing room
at the end of the night?

Music suddenly
a little too loud,
the ice returning
to water once more.

It's the idea
of facing
daylight alone—

a beaming cop
standing
at your window.
Do you know
how fast
you were going
back there?

If I could tell you
I would.
I would say
anything
to have you
on your way.

## Matinee

A stagehand bumps the flimsy wall and the poem collapses
like a house around Buster Keaton. Who in this room
needs to apologize for artifice? I do. Maybe it's that, for years,
I slept with the television on to drown out obsessive thoughts.
Life flipped before my eyes like a magazine, so now I'm here
staging one-act plays for the empty house. The stagehands
wheel the stucco buttresses away and begin to strike
the set. Each Potemkin Village is torn down
and carried off into storage. I have always been this way—
always lonely when the credits rolled. I'm not ready to leave
just yet. I stick around the theater, my feet kicked up
over the seat in front of me, my cigar still burning, leaving piles
of ash in the aisle. Houselights go up and I see the speckle
of confetti across the proscenium. An usher sweeps the debris
that remains, leaving me and my ash. When the usher's gone
I'm the last one left in the poem, and I'm a little afraid
to be here without anything else to distract me.

## Lunch in The Summer

*—after Stephen Duck*

The Lord is a painter.
Already he's retired certain colors—
set them aside to crumble
like the amusement park
on the edge of town,
gathering thistles.
But we still have green
in its many forms—
on lawns and boulevards,
under the noontime sun.
How I love lunch in the summer—
how good it feels to be allowed,
by law, to experience opulence:
sitting back in your car
in the Burger King parking lot,
food laid on your dashboard,
you become like a thresher
beneath a shady tree
three hundred years ago, scythe
nowhere in sight. Or, eating
a Caesar salad, you enjoy
the cool feeling of the porcelain plate
against your wrist and fingertips
as you graze it on the table.
Then it warms from your touch
and turns the temperature
of everything else.

## White Tower

Just before the promenade she turned
towards a chapel's yellowing sign
and said *maybe we should we just do it now*
right there on the deserted Niagara street,
still bereft of people on account of plague.
The city was still, as if an occupying force
had just withdrawn, and the mist plumed
in enormous columns, scaling higher
than the taupe casinos, the Rainforest Café,
or the Giacomo Hotel. In our room, I lay
in bed watching as dense fog eliminated the city
from sight. While she slept I swallowed
fiery thoughts. I shivered. I breathed. Anything
I could do to endure the fog so that maybe
the blinking tower could reveal itself again,
and then it did: its needle spire, its cascade of lights
signaling the existence of Canada, pouring in
through the hotel window
like theremin music through the dark.

JOSHUA MCKINNEY

**Joshua McKinney**'s fifth book of poetry, *Sad Animal* (Gunpowder Press, 2024), was the recipient of the John Ridland Poetry Prize. His work has appeared widely in such journals as *Boulevard, Denver Quarterly, Kenyon Review, New American Writing,* and *Ploughshares.* His other awards include The Dorothy Brunsman Poetry Prize, The Dickinson Prize, The Pavement Saw Chapbook Prize, and a Gertrude Stein Award for Innovative Writing. He is co-editor of the online ecopoetics magazine, *Clade Song.*

## World Enough

At the department meeting,
I am sitting, back to the wall,
in the back corner of the room,
next to the antique pencil-sharpener
bolted to the wall, its little crank
hanging down at six o'clock,
the hour it has tolled for years.
I am trying to remember Marvell's mistress,
but the lines are coy, coming
to me in pieces, which is, I suppose,
no crime. And there is, after all,
the assistance of rhyme. Now
I find that I am left complaining
by the "tide of Humber," and I wonder
how does it go from there?
Someone is making a motion
to make a motion on a previous
motion, concerning the minutes
from the last meeting, those precious
minutes forever lost, and, ah, yes,
here comes time's wingèd chariot,
with that memorable accented suffix,
interrupted by a cold blast of horns and
motors from the street outside. The Dean
is making a case for cancelling
a poetry class with only twenty-five students.
I suppose I am expected to object,
but the willing soul expires, no,

wait, *transpires*, and I would rather
this moment devour than languish
in the slow-chapped power
of this latest scheme: Tell us, in ten words
or less, why poetry is important,
and we will use it in a student recruitment
campaign on Twitter. I have lost
my youthful hue, it's true, yet
I can still seize these lines from
some recess of my brain, and find
sport amid these monthly deserts
of vast eternity, where I must tear
my pleasure through the iron gates
of budgetary strife. And now I hear
a blessèd movement to adjourn,
and rise to go, reminded yet again,
of the importance of poetry.

# Reap

The next fire, in the black weeds,

        whispers prayers for the last fire.

I can hear it hiss with slim tongues

        of green flame in the spring grass.

Soon, I ween that seeds of fire will spark a harvest,

        the brightest dark revelation.

# Homage to Thomas Traherne in the Pyrocene

*Manuscripts don't burn.*
        —Mikhail Bulgakov


On the road from Lancashire, a man saved God
        from a trash fire, where blackening pages
curled, the heat-cracked hydrocarbons unmade,
        then made again in destruction's bright image.

It was such heat and light drew my first eyes
        away from paradise. And when at last
I saw again, earth's beauty was ablaze
        beyond change. Candled in catastrophe, it cast

no promise of a further birth. I thought
        of all that had been lost, the hidden book
engulfed within each tree—how I was not
        recorded there—such immaculate lack as to wake

the glowing ember of God in a trash fire,
        or the incandescent soul of the late earth's pyre.

LEE HERRICK

**Lee Herrick** is the tenth California Poet Laureate and the first Asian American in the role. He is the author of *In Praise of Late Wonder: New and Selected Poems* (Gunpowder Press, 2024), as well as *Scar and Flower, Gardening Secrets of the Dead*, and *This Many Miles from Desire*. He co-edited *The World I Leave You: Asian American Poets on Faith and Spirit* and *Afterlives: An AGNI Portfolio of Asian Adoptee Diaspora Writing*. His poems appear in anthologies such as *Here: Poems for the Planet* (introduction by the Dalai Lama), and *Indivisible: Poems of Social Justice* (foreword by Common). Adopted as an infant from Daejeon, Korea, he lives and teaches in Fresno, California.

# In Praise of Late Wonder

I've wondered what my Korean mother's voice
sounded like when I was born. Was it gasp, hiss,
or flag in light wind? I've wondered if she kissed
me before I became a wind, a white noise
in blue sky. I've wondered lately about joy.
Butterfly, hummingbird, angels so full of bliss
they almost sing. I imagine some of this
relates to the orphan I was, the adopted boys
and girls like me, all diaspora and alarm.
I've wondered if I'm made of smoke and fire.
Sometimes, clear sky. Sometimes, quiet storm.
I've wondered lately how the acoustic guitar
keeps its secrets, makes me float a little higher.
How could I not love looking at the stars?

Acclimation

My first language was the ocean.
It sounded like my first mother's
body: wave, storm, vanish.

I love what the wind does
to the trees. I want nature
to move me like that.

My name is a song. In it,
there are horses, fed by a man
who says I feel American when I kill

a row of ants and say they asked for it.
We are this many miles from desire.
We are immigrant turned imperialist.

I love what the wind does to the bay.
Wave to me. Smile at me
like you know my name,

like you love the ocean, too,
or at least the way
I glisten in the starlight.

## The Time I Spent Inside a Star

How could I not love looking at the stars?
Once, I dreamt that I climbed inside of one.
It was darker than you'd think, but still fun
enough to feel like astronomy. There was a bar
serving drinks mixed with cosmic dust, bizarre
but delicious. It felt like a kind of heaven,
like I imagine California or Daejeon.
I want to read my birth mother's memoir.
To remember is an attempt to be free.
The time I spent inside a star,
I've wondered how to best believe
it was real. It was no more a dream
than I am alive and have made it this far,
dust-covered, full of joy, evergreen.

## Partial Crown in Praise of Absent Sounds

I want the fax machine, the dot matrix
buzz saw of news across the wire,
the young woman's lisp and fire
during solo moonlight road trips,
the shuffle of predictable card tricks,
the acoustic chord like sweet desire,
the rotary dial and pronunciation error.
When I say absent sounds, I mean
typewriter key as much as aniyo or ye,
the 8-track plunk as much as Korean
vowels drawn out at the end like a plain
blue sky. I want to know the way
home. There's not much more I need.

Home. There's not much more I need
except to know how much blue sky
there is from here to you, why
I sometimes hear your voice freed,
wild, true. Please, take the lead.
At times, I thought I was going to die.
At times, fire. At other times, firefly.
My daughter was four at the art gallery
and called it the art galaxy, a malapropism
I wish existed: star, sonnet, serenade.
I want the mispronunciation, broken rhythm
and scratched record. Survivor wisdom.
A mother's prayer for her son, who stayed
perfectly still when she left and kissed him.

SM Stubbs

**SM Stubbs** lives in Brooklyn, NY, where he and his wife co-owned a craft-beer bar. Born and raised in South Florida, he attended Wake Forest and then Indiana University where he received his MFA. He was the recipient of a scholarship to and on staff at Bread Loaf Writers' Conference and was nominated for the Pushcart Prize and Best New Poets. His work has appeared in *Poetry Northwest, Poem-A-Day, New Ohio Review, december, Iron Horse, The Rumpus, Crab Creek Review, Cagibi, Anacapa Review* and elsewhere.

## Asylum Sleight of Hand

In order to escape you must know the sounds
        for *trap* and *fettered flesh*. You must allow yourself

to be audacious, a name for a type of dare. This
        is a lesson in embracing the other. To start with,

stop apologizing for the spoiled hull of your body.
        Next, learn to get away with what doesn't belong

to you: starlight, the smell of jasmine, the weight
        of hollow bones called a wing. Death is either

reprieve or release. When our judgment ends
        we are free to never eat, never sleep, never learn

the geometry of any lover's extended sentence,
        their pliable curves and neon stitches. Do you

have the nerve? A lab on the south of town
        proves that risk-taking is good for our health,

that it energizes us like a fresh set of electrodes.
        Whatever holds you eventually loosens its grip.

## Asylum Linguistics

It turns out the word "fornicate" used to mean
        an arched or vaulted form, as if two bodies

bent by heat could carry the weight of the sky.
        One root suggests "brothel," another means

a "domed shape" or "covered way." Roman
        prostitutes solicited business under the arches

of certain buildings which is why one author
        of the bible linked the location to adultery.

I'd ask him about the importance of contact,
        skin to skin, the manner in which we most

reveal ourselves. I'd ask him if he knew how
        to define love or the four elements of a fractured

selfhood. I'd tell him: we are poisoned through
        our mouths, the center of half our sins. Without

evidence we don't really know what we know.
        How far will we fall? As far as language allows.

## Asylum Release

We're scarred, but not all scars are created equal.
      It can be helpful to come at it from a surprising angle,

i.e., the wire caught in that branch is the same color
      as the wire he tied my hands with. Understand,

the heart wants to share its pain with another heart.
      If not share, inflict. This the blues. This

the stretched-out forever ahead. Dolor on the hi-fi,
      guitar and harmonies like a soul on fire. A loss.

A wound. A scab you carry inside. Bruises and lacerations
      are fine if inflicted at significant moments:

a lover's teeth, a father's belt buckle, a mother's wine glass
      opening the smooth landscape of your flesh.

In the empty after: the challenge of the body sacred.
      No one wants to ruin their childhood yet these thick

chains clatter with every step. First, you must admit
      the child you were wasn't sure what wanting meant.

## The Spoils

The thing is, you have Paris and California
and all I have is this bird. It shits
non-stop, and when I said
I wanted to remember you, I meant
your mouth scented with wine and your calves
as they tipped you up to kiss me and even
the embrace of your sighs. It may be
too much to ask, I know. I left you
the stereo and big-screen TV; I left you
the Polish landlord who loved wrestling; I left you
the platform bed you never really liked—
and not one of those defecates in your cereal.
Justice isn't made to partner love. None of this
is how it was meant to go. There were times
we held each other when there was nowhere else
in the world, but that was long ago.
Now I'm nauseous twenty-four seven
and my dreams twitch with the metal twang
of your chinchillas in their cages, so many
sleepless nights. There are days when I wish
this bird had been a vampire bat with plans
to drain me of vital essences. There are other days
when I wish it was a Guanay cormorant—
their feces tend to explode. Either way
I imagine me up after midnight scraping guano
from the furniture and floors, learning
how to extract the potassium nitrate, me burning
our table and chairs for charcoal. I imagine
buying sulfur at the garden center,
mixing it in a huge bucket.
I take that crude gunpowder and lace
our past with it. I strike a match, prepared
to fly. I let the flame go and act like those fireworks
have nothing to do with love, or ruin, or me.

HOLLY KARAPETKOVA

**Holly Karapetkova** is Poet Laureate Emerita of Arlington, Virginia, and a recipient of a 2022 Academy of American Poets Laureate Fellowship for her work with young poets. Her poetry, prose, and translations have appeared widely in print and online. She is the author of two books of poetry, *Towline*, winner of the Vern Rutsala Poetry Prize from Cloudbank Books, and *Words We Might One Day Say*, winner of the Washington Writers' Publishing House Prize for Poetry. She lives in Arlington, Virginia, and teaches at Marymount University.

# Dear White Girl

Dear errata. Apology. Dear sugar and spice, cherry and cherry pop. Dear pillar of salt, pillar of the plantation, love and charity to all. Dear Barbie doll in a permanent ball gown, Barbie Dream House and who'd she have to marry to end up there. Dear laurel tree and hollow reeds. Dear sorrow-become-stone, caged-in-the-forest, turned-into-a-bird. Dear picked flowers, wild and domesticated. Dear Wyoming and Louisiana and 81 cents to the dollar. Dear Scylla and Charybdis, Good Witches of the North and South, Governor's wife, Overseer's wife, CEO's wife, slumlord's wife. I didn't mean what I said. Please don't let me end up with that old maid card in my hand.

## Still Life

I always wanted to be
a good girl, white
as a canvas,
a knuckled grip.

This meant holding
my breath.
This meant
counting to ten

or ten thousand,
watching
all the lights
in the city

for something
to flicker:
a secret message,
a passage out.

Nothing ever appeared
but a distant flash
of lightning,
roadside sign

with its mouth
full of neon
blinking
XXX

silence,
the shadows of white
roses darkening the sidewalk.

## Dear Empire

Blue-eyed wonder of the universe,
you have all the answers.

If you stopped breathing
the world would wheeze to a stop—

milky way run out of milk,
solar system spit out its moons,

rivers stop running bereft
of so many bodies.

No one can wreck
without your wrecking ball,

shoot without your 6-gauge,
piss without your chamber pot.

Though you paid fair market value
this land is not yours.

Though its denizens break
their backs for your paltry wage

their minds are running
toward their own horizon

where the sun rises,
a light you can't steal.

## There Are Boats

There are boats
and people sail them
out to sea
out past the sight of land
across an ocean
full of sharks.

There are boats
and people on them
far out at sea
deep in the pockets
of a gathering storm.

There are boats
that sink
and boats that float
boats made of
metal and wood
and boats made
of inflatable plastic

full of children
full of mothers
floating with nothing
but what they could carry
carrying nothing
but the air beneath them.

KEITH EKISS

**Keith Ekiss** is a former Wallace Stegner Fellow at Stanford University. In addition to *Burial Fragments* (Gunpowder Press, 2025, winner of the Barry Spacks Poetry Prize), he is the author of *Pima Road Notebook* and translator of two books by the Costa Rican poet Eunice Odio: *The Fire's Journey*, an epic poem in four volumes; and *Territory of Dawn: The Selected Poems of Eunice Odio*. He is the past recipient of fellowships and residencies from the Bread Loaf Writers' Conference, Community of Writers' Conference, Millay Colony for the Arts, Santa Fe Art Institute, and the Petrified Forest National Park.

# Burial Fragments

*—Buena Vista Park*

There's no room for the dead

in this small city, nearly an island,
where we trade corpses for houses

digging up graves
and disturbing the bones.

You can die in San Francisco,
but you can't keep the real estate.

On a path toward the hospital,
gutters laid from headstones,

names split from dates.
I visit to read fragments,

cursive of another century
spelling out a memory:

*Frances, loving Mother.*
Many names I'll never find.

They were turned to face the earth.

## Target Practice

A Sunday morning voice
behind the door I'd just opened
said she was selling
the *Socialist Review*

and asked if I wasn't ready
*to take up arms for the revolution.*
I offered a dollar
and the conversation turned

to capitalism: she worked
part-time, didn't vote, and spent
her afternoons on the firing range
taking practice shots

at President Clinton.
I'd never held a handgun,
and she wanted me to learn.
The workers were uniting,

but I wanted coffee and the paper,
no matter what my comrade said.
I don't believe in revolution,
but I often want to let the stranger in.

## Flowers and Runaways

Street teens repeat the standard line: *Spare change for bud?* Who sleeps
in a park, who sleeps in a suburb, the shirt's the same: *Green Day.* You
lived at Haight and Ashbury, the house without a gate, and stepped over
junkies sprawled on a welcome mat, gloving your hand to retrieve their
needles. Sunday mornings, hung over, you slipped out to buy coffee
and bagels, to breathe the park air and soak up the fog, its democratic
calm, what you shared with those teens besides the angel's trumpets,
pendulous bell that calls an eye to see and a mouth to taste its poison.

# Boy

He mimics. And drinks ungodly volumes of milk.
*Again, again*
he cries to hear the book about a dog who plays flute,
laughing like a drunk at jokes he doesn't get.

He overhears the rain like a conversation
and murmurs to himself, not like a lonely man,
but one amused by genius. He doesn't know
heaven or death. Too young to spot hummingbirds,

too old to swaddle like a mummy.
Words appear in his mouth from the air.
He's got no reason to believe
a dog can't speak.

**Kellam Ayres:** Prior to publication in *In the Cathedral of My Undoing*, "Summer" appeared in *B O D Y*

**Aaron Baker:** Prior to publication in *Posthumous Noon*, "The Infernal Regions," appeared in *Poetry Northwest*; "Dark Matter" appeared in *Missouri Review*.

**Christopher Blackman:** Prior to publication in *Three-Day Weekend*, "Lunch in the Summer" appeared in *Open Space.*

**Nan Cohen:** Prior to publication in *Unfinished City*, the poem "In the Unfinished City" appeared in *Jews*; "Ordeals by Water" appeared in *Grasslands Review.*

**Todd Copeland:** Prior to publication in *Like All Light* "The Cast Line" appeared in *The Journal*; "Jefferson River Road" appeared in the chapbook *The Book as Knife* (Ravenna Press); "Glimpsed" appeared in *Relief: A Journal of Art and Faith*; "Nine Mile Mountain" appeared in *Valparaiso Poetry Review.*

**Meghan Dunn:** Prior to publication in *Curriculum*, "Historical Context: Two Lesson Plans" appeared in *Southern Humanities Review*

**Keith Ekiss:** Prior to publication in *Burial Fragments,* the poem "Burial Fragments" appeared in *The Cincinnati Review*; "Target Practice" and "Flowers and Runaways" in *The Southern Review*; "Boy" appeared in *Meridian.*

**Michelle Bonczek Evory:** Prior to publication in *The Ghosts of Lost Animals*, "Yaquina Bay, and Darkness" was published in *Weber—The Contemporary West* and received the Dr. Sherwin W. Howard Award for poetry in 2011.

**Glenn Freeman:** Prior to publication in *Drinking with O'Hara*, "On Moving One More Time" appeared in *Able Muse*; "14 Notebook Fragments After My Mother Died" appeared in *Under a Warm Green Linden*; "Oh Yeah!" appeared in *Main Street Rag.*

**Lee Herrick:** Prior to publication in In Praise of Late Wonder, the poem "In Praise of Late Wonder" appeared in *Hanging Loose*; "Acclimation" appeared in *Huizache*; "Partial Crown in Praise of Absent Sounds" appeared in *San Diego Poetry Annual*.

**Catherine Abbey Hodges:** Prior to publication in *Empty Me Full*, "Old Blue Shirt" appeared in *SALT;* "By Which I Mean Repent" appeared in *Gyroscope Review*.

**Holly Karapetkova:** Prior to publication in *Dear Empire*, "Dear White Girl" appeared in *This is What America Looks Like: Poetry and Fiction from D.C., Maryland, and Virginia*; "Dear Empire" appeared in *Alaska Quarterly Review*; "There are Boats" appeared in *Blackbird*.

**Susan Kelly-DeWitt:** Prior to publication in *Gatherer's Alphabet*, "Narcissus" appeared in *Prairie Schooner;* "Calling the Horses" appeared in *Morning Thunder Poems* (Plumas County Arts Commission). Prior to publication in *Frangible Operas*, "Teaching Poetry in the Prisons" was published in *Writers Resist*.

**Joshua McKinney:** Note on "Homage to Thomas Traherne in the Pyrocene": In 1967, the manuscript of Thomas Traherne's *Commentaries of Heaven* was rescued from a burning rubbish heap in England by a man looking for car parts.

**Sandra McPherson:** Prior to publication in *Speech Crush*, the poem "Speech Crush" appeared in *Poetry;* "Current, Matadero Creek" appeared in *Crazyhorse*; "After Trauma" appeared in *Ploughshares*.

**Kurt Olsson:** Prior to publication in *Buring Down Disneyland*, "Just Once" appeared in *Passages North;* "The Stars Are Too Far to Need Faces" appeared in *Mid-American Review*.

**Jim Peterson:** Prior to publication in *Original Face*, "Other Laws for the People" was included in the chapbook *The Resolution of Eve* (Finishing Line Press); "No News" appeared in *Southern Poetry Review*.

**Catherine Esposito Prescott:** The poem "Accidental Garden" is an American sentence acrostic, a poetic form created by the poet's brilliant friend, Jen Karetnick. The American sentence acrostic takes a 17-syllable American sentence, as defined by Allen Ginsberg, and uses it as an acrostic to build a poem. Prior to publication in *Accidental Garden*, the poem "Accidental Garden" appeared in *Mezzo Cammin*; "Instructions: Our Next Lifetime" appeared in *Northwest Review*; "Ode" appeared in *SWWIM + Womanish*.

**Peg Quinn:** Prior to publication in Mother Lode, "Spring Planting" was published in *Nebraska Life Magazine*.

**Dennis Schmitz:** Prior to publication in *Our Music*, "Two-Beer Ethics" appeared in *Hubbub*; "Systems" and "The Other Side" appeared in *Field*; "80ᵗʰ Birthday" *Cloudbank*.

**Barry Spacks:** Prior to publication in *Shaping Water*, "What Breathes Us" and "Whitewater Vision" were included in *The Hope of the Air* (Michigan State University Press, 2004).

**SM Stubbs:** Prior to publication in *Learning to Drown*, "Asylum Sleight of Hand" appeared in *Menacing Hedge*; "Asylum Linguistics" appeared in *Variant Literature*; "Asylum Release"appeared in *Raleigh Review*; "The Spoils" appeared in *Jabberwock*.

# Barry Spacks Poetry Prize

2024   *Dear Empire*, by Holly Karapetkova
       *Burial Fragments*, by Keith Ekiss

2023   Gary Soto, final judge
       *In the Cathedral of My Undoing*, by Kellam Ayres

2022   Danusha Laméris, final judge
       *Accidental Garden*, by Catherine Esposito Prescott

2021   Lynne Thompson, final judge
       *Like All Light*, by Todd Copeland

2020   Jessica Jacobs, final judge
       *Curriculum*, by Meghan Dunn

2019   Stephen Dunn, final judge
       *Drinking with O'Hara*, by Glenn Freeman

2018   Lee Herrick, final judge
       *The Ghosts of Lost Animals*, by Michelle Bonczek Evory

2017   Jane Hirshfield, final judge
       *Posthumous Noon*, by Aaron Baker

2016   Thomas Lux, final judge
       *Burning Down Disneyland*, by Kurt Olsson

2015   Dan Gerber, final judge
       *Instead of Sadness*, by Catherine Abbey Hodges

## Gunpowder Press
# California Poets Series

*In Praise of Late Wonder*, poems by Lee Herrick

*Downtime*, poems by Gary Soto

*Speech Crush*, poems by Sandra McPherson

*Our Music*, poems by Dennis Schmitz

*Gatherer's Alphabet*, poems by Susan Kelly-DeWitt

# Alta California Chapbooks
### Emma Trelles, Series Editor

*Alba and Other Songs*, poems by Fred Arroyo

*The First Amelia*, poems by Amelia Rodriguez

*On Display*, poems by Gabriel Ibarra

*Sor Juana*, poems by Florencia Milito

*Levitations*, poems by Nicholas Reiner

*Grief Logic*, poems by Crystal AC Salas

GUNPOWDER PRESS

# SHORELINE VOICES SERIES
celebrating poetic voices in our community

*Women in a Golden State:*
*California Poets at 60 and Beyond*
Edited by Diana Raab & Chryss Yost

*Out of the Ground:*
*Poems Inspired by Santa Barbara Botanic Garden*
Edited by David Starkey & Chryss Yost

*While You Wait:*
*A Collection by Santa Barbara County Poets*
Edited by Laure-Anne Bosselaar

*To Give Life a Shape:*
*Poems Inspired by the Santa Barbara Museum of Art*
Edited by David Starkey & Chryss Yost

*What Breathes Us:*
*Santa Barbara Poets Laureate, 2005-2015*
Edited by David Starkey

*Rare Feathers: Poems on Birds & Art*
Edited by Nancy Gifford, Chryss Yost,
& George Yatchisin

*Buzz: Poets Respond to SWARM*
Edited by Nancy Gifford & Chryss Yost

# Dryden-Vreeland Book Prize

honoring poets working in K-12 education

*Three-Day Weekend*
Poems by Christopher Blackman

*Unfinished City*
Poems by Nan Cohen

# Also from Gunpowder Press

*The Tarnation of Faust*: Poems by David Case

*Mouth & Fruit*: Poems by Chryss Yost

*Shaping Water*: Poems by Barry Spacks

*Original Face*: Poems by Jim Peterson

*Raft of Days*: Poems by Catherine Abbey Hodges

*Mother Lode*: Poems by Peg Quinn

*Before Traveling to Alabama*: Poems by David Case

*Frangible Operas*: Poems by Susan Kelly-DeWitt

*Empty Me Full*: Poems by Catherine Abbey Hodges

*Learning to Drown*: Poems by SM Stubbs

www.ingramcontent.com/pod-product-compliance
Lightning Source LLC
Chambersburg PA
CBHW020254130626
46549CB00005B/2208

*9 7 8 1 9 5 7 0 6 2 2 2 8 *